ITALIAN RIVIERA

By the staff of Editions Berlitz

Reprinted 1981

Library of Congress Catalog Card Number:
78-52517.

Berlitz Trademark Reg. U.S. Patent Office
and other countries – Marca Registrada.

Printed in Switzerland by Weber SA, Bienne

Preface

A new kind of travel guide for the jet age—Berlitz has packed all you need to know about the Italian Riviera into this compact and colourful book, one of an extensive series on the world's top tourist areas.

Like our phrase books and dictionaries, this book fits your pocket—in both size and price. It also aims to fit your travel needs:

- It concentrates on your specific destination—the Italian Riviera—not an entire country.

- It combines easy reading with fast facts: what to see and do, where to shop, what to eat.

- An authoritative A-to-Z "blueprint" fills the back of the book, giving clear-cut answers to all your questions, from "How much does it cost to rent a car?" to "How do I make a long-distance call?"—plus how to get there and when to go.

- Easy-to-read maps in full colour, dividing the coast into convenient areas, pinpoint sights you'll want to see.

In short, this handy guide will help you enjoy your visit to the Italian Riviera. From the Renaissance palaces of Genoa to the sleek yachts of Portofino, from snorkelling to spaghetti factories, Berlitz tells you clearly and concisely what it's all about.

Let your travel agent help you choose a hotel. Let a restaurant guide help you choose a good place to eat. But to decide "What should we do today?" travel with Berlitz.

Photography: Jean-Claude Vieillefond
We're particularly grateful to Don Larrimore, Barbara Norton and Mary Nicholson for their help with the preparation of this book. We also wish to thank the Italian National Tourist Office and the Azienda Autonoma di Turismo for their valuable assistance.

4 🔹 Cartography: Falk-Verlag, Hamburg

Contents

How to use this guide
If time is short, look for items to visit which are printed in bold type in this book, e.g. the **Caves of Toirano.** Those sights most highly recommended are not only given in bold type but also carry our traveller symbol, e.g. **San Remo.**

The Land and the People

A sweeping, sun-splashed semicircle, arching some 160 miles along the Mediterranean from France to Tuscany—this is the Italian Riviera. Rocky cover, sandy beaches and towering promontories punctuate the shoreline. Luxuriant resorts and little fishing ports share the verdant landscape of this region, officially known as Liguria, with mountain villages where little has changed for centuries. At the heart of it all is the venerable maritime centre of Genoa.

Genoa, in fact, divides the coast in two: the Riviera di Levante (of the rising sun) stretches to the east and south, the Riviera di Ponente (the setting sun), westward to the French border. The sheltering Alps and Apennines ensure temperate weather almost all year long; the juxtaposition of sea and mountain creates constant air currents that enable farmers to grow four vegetable crops a year.

Much more than the benign

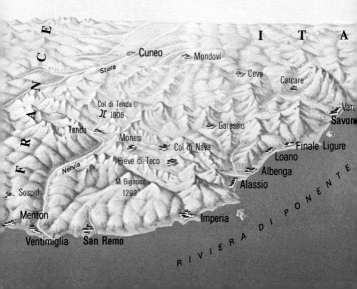

climate attracts visitors and compels so many to return or stay. Certainly there's the enchanting spectacle of natural beauty. In spring, Riviera slopes are carpeted with almond, peach and apricot blossom; yellow mimosa flowers everywhere and you can walk beside fields of roses and carnations. Olive groves render some of the world's finest oil, vineyards some entirely satisfactory wines. Orange and lemon trees, eucalyptus and cypress add to the opulent setting. Every village has its church of solemn beauty, the tiniest hamlet a watchtower or a Roman bridge, a *castello,* archways, narrow old lanes.

And, of course, there's the Mediterranean. Along the meandering shoreline the sea pounds against rocks or runs hissing up long beaches, playing castanets with the shingle. Countless inlets harbour boats of all descriptions; nowadays you'll see mostly pleasure craft, but sturdy workaday boats weigh anchor, too.

Fishermen, whose craggy faces mirror their ancient Ligurian heritage, no longer catch what they used to. Most fish

seek the sea's depths where the water is purer—but the work isn't quite as hard now with labour-saving aids. You may see nets strung out from beaches behind boats, then dragged ashore by whole families wearing traditional canvas backbands to help them heave.

Nearly 2 million people live in Liguria, including a rather large number of foreigners and

A touch of music, sun and good humour make up a Ligurian holiday.

recent settlers from other parts of Italy. The natives, more serious and aloof than most Mediterraneans, have a reputation for thrift that has started legends. But beneath that exterior you'll find great warmth and patience. These people have resisted invasion over the centuries, their towns occupied often but never totally conquered. In turn, they have sent off mariners and explorers around the world and produced a wealth of enduring art.

Local customs perplex some visitors. Natives don't often wait patiently in a queue—it's simply not part of their character. Radios and television sets

seem unalterably to be turned on to full volume, and even then may hardly be heard over the conversations. On the other hand, everyone says *buon giorno* (before lunch) and *buona sera* (after siesta) when entering and leaving a bar or shop, even if they're ignored in the general hubbub. And in the extravagant Italian fashion, parents pamper their offspring.

You can dine simply and abundantly at scores of *trattorie,* along the Riviera, but if you're looking for exquisite food in romantic settings where only the moon intrudes on your table, you'll also find that. Some of the best dishes in Italy's gastronomical spectrum are Ligurian creations.

The Riviera is not a *mañana* land: the native and imported Ligurians are far too lively for that. Service is generally fast and considerate. Modern-living adjuncts seem to work: the electricity doesn't fail as often as in many Mediterranean paradises, trains run more or less on time, buses are conveniently routed to provide good regular service, minor roads, even up into the mountains, are well-paved and, with few exceptions, well-marked, museums open and close at the stated hours, films and concerts begin almost on schedule. All the efficiency does not discourage relaxation —you can, if you wish, eat late into the night, for example, and the three-hour afternoon siesta, that eminently sensible hot-weather tradition, still exists on the Riviera.

A sleek *autostrada* with a dizzying series of tunnels and viaducts slices the Riviera in two. Far slower and less impersonal is the twisting Via Aurelia, paved and occasionally widened but otherwise scarcely changed from the days when it was the longest road the Romans ever built.

This famous coast is no longer a retreat for the privileged few. Happily, signs of that change have been kept pretty much within bounds. The charming towns have not been disfigured by concrete superstructures. More people, yes, but more facilities too. There are plenty of reasonably priced hotels and guest houses, deck chairs, pedal, sailing or motor boats. The Riviera offers scenic mountains, a sparkling sea, sunny skies, fine food and above all, a multitude of enthusiastic, hospitable people.

Far from the madding crowd, turquoise waters in a tranquil cove.

10

A Brief History

Dramatic topography has meant dramatic history for Liguria. Though its severe mountain backdrop made passage from the hinterland difficult, Liguria was wide open to attacks from the sea and, over the centuries, was invaded time and again.

First on the scene were the Ligurians who gave the region its name, driven from Alpine regions by the Celts. The present-day inhabitants trace their ancestry back to these primitive fishermen and coastal traders, who mixed with hill tribes.

Invariably, the story of Liguria has depended on the changing fortunes of its premier port, Genoa. As far back as the 5th century B.C., Genoa was a respectable-sized metropolis in commercial contact with the Greeks and Etruscans (as proved by archaeological finds in the rich necropolis by

Evocative ruins near Andora draw tourists away from the beach.

A

CRISTOFORO COLOMBO

LA PATRIA

Via XX Settembre). When Rome launched her policy of far-ranging expansionism in the 3rd century B.C., she was quick to realize the strategic advantage of Genoa and its rivieras. At first relations were friendly, but in due course (222 B.C.) Rome gained control of the region. Traces of the Roman fortresses, built to discourage tribal upheavals, can still be seen. Genoa and other fine Ligurian harbours became bases for Roman vessels.

Genoa was sacked—for the first of many times—in 205 B.C. by the Carthaginians (supposedly led by Hannibal's brother). The Romans then erected a larger town around the prized harbour. Even after the empire fell in the 5th century A.D., Genoa and smaller Riviera ports like La Spezia, Camogli, Savona, Varigotti and Albenga continued to develop as trading stations. But they also feuded violently among themselves and were too weak to repulse invasions by foreign marauders.

Another foe came from North Africa: the Moors or Saracens who destroyed Genoa in 936. Under the leadership of the pope, the Genoese joined forces with Pisa in the next century to assault the Saracen island strongholds of Corsica and Sardinia.

The Genoese Empire

After the defeat of the Saracens in 1148, Genoa became the foremost power in the Mediterranean, a title Pisa disputed in a long series of wars. Little by little Genoa gained hold of the Ligurian coast and most of Corsica and set up its first maritime trading posts. Victory over Pisa in the naval battle of Meloria (1284) cleared the way for Genoa to reign supreme. The city's population swelled to about 100,000—huge for the times—making it one of medieval Europe's largest centres.

Even during the Crusades in the 11th and 12th centuries, the Genoese had not been reluctant to do business with the Moslems of the Turkish empire. Their boats carried cargoes from the eastern Mediterranean, through the Straits of Gibraltar to northern Europe. Now competing primarily against Venice, Genoa set up some important colonies in the Crimea, Syria, Greece and

One Genoan who ventured far beyond the borders of his hometown.

15

North Africa. (Christopher Columbus, incidentally, came from Genoa, though he sailed under the Spanish flag.)

On the home front, however, the Ligurians were disunited, beset by political turbulence and foreign intrusion. A stable and lasting administrative set-up seemed to elude them. Local consuls elected annually in the 12th century gave way to city managers *(podestà)* brought in from outside. After successive invasions by the French and others, 1339 saw Genoa taken over by Simon Boccanegra, the first in a line of doges, theoretically absolute, lifetime rulers who ran their territories through subservient councils.

Guelphs and Ghibellines

Unfortunately, tyranny did not mean tranquillity. Genoa was racked for generations by internecine disputes related to the struggle between the papacy and the Holy Roman Emperors. On the one side were the Guelph families (supporters of the pope)—the Fieschi, Grimaldi and Guarchi; on the other, their Ghibelline rivals—the Doria, Adorno, Spinola and Fregoso. Through it all, the feuding families managed to amass vast fortunes, building elegant palaces in Genoa and opulent villas along the Levante and Ponente rivieras. Art, sculpture and architecture flourished, though not on the lavish scale of Milan or Florence. The Genoese became highly adept mapmakers. They also developed new financial activities, such as marine insurance and commercial banking; their banks had provided much of the money for the Crusades.

These skills became critically important as Genoa's empire began to decline. From 1346 to 1348 a severe epidemic of the "Black Death" ravaged Liguria. Bitter economic rivalries led to further fragmentation: the coast was dotted with hilltop castles *(castelli)* and fortified towns. Local nobles, real or self-created, often allied with the Catholic church to strengthen their position. Commune-style government was tried for a period but failed, and still more feudal fiefdoms sprang up.

Overseas, Genoa gradually lost its eastern Mediterranean colonies and long-distance shipping contracts. Defeat at the hands of Venice in the war of Chioggia (1378–81) signalled the end of Genoa's maritime supremacy.

In the late 14th and early 15th centuries, new rulers—

such as Charles VI of France and the Milanese—swept in to seize control of Liguria's productive vineyards and olive groves, deep harbours and improved roads leading to the interior. The Milanese intervened both by invitation and without it, and several more French kings launched attacks on the beleaguered coastal strip. Genoa endured 14 revolutions within 40 years and was brutally sacked in 1522 by the Spanish army. Decline into oblivion seemed inevitable.

Financial Renaissance

Instead, Liguria's fortunes rebounded remarkably. The surprising reversal began on September 13, 1528, when Admiral Andrea Doria passed through the battered walls of Genoa to be welcomed as a saviour by the weary population. Formerly in the service of France, Doria had broken away and made an arrangement with Holy Roman Emperor Charles V, guaranteeing the city's independence. Genoa's most-beloved local hero and Italy's most-revered admiral, he gave the city an oligarchic constitution and re-established peace for a time on the Riviera—no mean feat.

Back in the early 15th century, at one of the darkest points in Genoa's history, a group of local merchants had created the Banco di San Giorgio. Originally involved in money changing, it grew during the century into a major financial power in the world. The city's bankers entrenched themselves at key points in the Spanish empire, including Antwerp and the Americas, using new techniques to assume control of the monetary networks of most trade of the Western world. These men, from Genoa's patrician families, had early perfected the art of credit. Now they became the indispensable masters of goods and currency exchange and commercial contracts.

Spain's kings, particularly Philip II, raised money for ambitious foreign undertakings almost exclusively through Genoa, the world's leading financial city in the second half of the 16th century. Milan, Venice and Florence all fell by the fiscal wayside. Silver, brought back by Spanish galleons from the Western hemisphere, was funnelled first to Genoa for distribution around Europe and the Mediterranean. In 1608 Genoa was able to become a free port. Its traditional nickname, "La Superba", was never more appropriate. **17**

Only as the 17th century advanced did the Portuguese begin to supplant the Genoese at the summit of international banking.

Forceful intervention in Genoa's affairs from outside continued. In 1684, Louis XIV of France bombarded Genoa and entered it without a struggle. Half a century later the Austrians, who had formed an alliance with Spain, occupied Liguria and imposed a cruelly oppressive regime. When they were eventually driven out, a teenage boy called Balilla became a local legend by being the first to throw a stone at the Austrian troops, sparking the successful popular resistance. Corsica, always restive under the protracted Genoese rule, was sold to France in 1768.

Some 30 years later, Napoleon Bonaparte, a rising young general of the new French Republic, crossed the Alps and defeated the Austrians who controlled northern Italy. After a siege in 1796, Genoa itself was taken and became part of the "Ligurian Republic". The French attempted to introduce revolutionary concepts of liberty, equality and brotherhood into the feudal domains along the coast. In the wake of Napoleon's downfall, the Ligurian Republic passed into history, and in 1815 the region was absorbed by the Kingdom of Sardinia.

Genoa and Italy

As the Italian peninsula struggled toward freedom and unification in the decades after 1814, Genoa became a major centre of political activism. A prime source of inspiration for this Risorgimento (reawakening) was Giuseppe Mazzini (1805–72), another illustrious Genoese who orchestrated the campaign for a unified Italy free of foreign domination. And from the Genoese suburb of Quarto, Giuseppe Garibaldi (1807–82) set sail in May 1860 with a thousand "Red Shirt" volunteers on his famous expedition to overthrow the Bourbon dynasty ruling Sicily and southern Italy. These two men, together with Count Camillo Cavour in Turin, are nationally revered as leaders of the movement which finally achieved the unification of Italy under Victor Emmanuel II of Piedmont in 1861 and took Rome as well in 1870. From then on, Genoa's port and industrial output became steadily more important for the entire peninsula.

Italy entered World War I in May 1915 on the side of Britain and France, holding the

Giuseppe Garibaldi set sail from Genoa with "Red Shirt" volunteers.

front against Germany's Austro-Hungarian allies in the Dolomites for 2½ years. A political journalist wounded there, Benito Mussolini (1883–1945), returned to Milan and began organizing *fasci* (groups) of working men to agitate for social reform. In March 1919 these groups became the Fascist party.

Italy was in a virtual state of civil war from February 1921 until October 1922, when Victor Emmanuel III appointed Mussolini prime minister. **19**

As *duce*, Mussolini assumed dictatorial powers. The war he launched against Abyssinia (1935–36) and his intervention in the Spanish Civil War on the side of Franco helped push Italy into the camp of Hitler's Germany.

Waves of resistance to fascism had coursed through Genoa from the early days of Mussolini's rule. After Italy joined Germany in World War II in 1940, the Genoese became more openly hostile, ultimately taking part in a successful uprising in April 1945, before the country's formal liberation by the Allies. Mussolini himself was captured and shot by partisans near Lake Como.

In 1946, Italians voted in referendum to replace the monarchy with the democratic republic which exists today. Genoa, badly damaged by wartime naval and air bombardment, was soon reconstructed and ever since has been Italy's leading seaport. The city contributed largely to the nation's considerable postwar economic boom. It has endured the effects of continuing political instability and with the rest of the Riviera has prospered from the latest, but this time peaceful, foreign invasion—of tourists.

What to See

Genoa *(Genova)*
Pop. 800,000

With its many kilometres of wharves berthing a steady stream of ships from around the world, Genoa easily convinces you that it has been one of the great ports of the Mediterranean for a thousand years. As giant loading cranes swing back and forth, marine brokers, customs officials, importers and exporters dart in and out of the often grandiose buildings of international steamship companies. From passenger piers here you can catch a ferry to Corsica and Sardinia, a cruise liner around the Mediterranean or farther afield.

Rising from the waterfront is one of Europe's hilliest cities. Some 800,000 Genoese live and work in this patchwork of palaces, boulevards and alleyways, medieval churches and modern office or apartment blocks. Street tunnels abound. More often than not in Genoa, a walk becomes a climb.

But walking is rewarding:

The old town—an intriguing maze of narrow lanes and tall houses.

Genoa's **old town** *(Centro Storico)*, particularly, contains many delights for the visitor. Extending along dockside from Via Gramsci (not to be visited at night!) to Via San Lorenzo and Piazza de Ferrari, the quarter is a maze of lanes *(carugi)* and steps, of tiny but tall houses and enormous palaces.

Two handsome and historic thoroughfares are the pride of the Genoese: **Via Balbi** and **Via Garibaldi.** Happily, they're unhilly. From the Principe railway station, you might cross Piazza Acquaverde and enter Via Balbi, designed at the beginning of the 17th century by the great Genoese architect, Bartolomeo Bianco. At No. 10 is the **Palazzo Balbi Durazzo** (formerly Palazzo Reale), perhaps the finest of the string of handsome palaces lining this street. Known as the Royal Palace, it was built in 1650 for the powerful but non-regal Balbi family (who also commissioned the street itself). Your lingering memory will surely be of the sumptuous decoration of the palace's rooms, the glowing colours of the tapestries, the pastel delicacy of the frescoes and of Van Dyck's commanding *Crucifixion.* The Hall of Mirrors is particularly elegant. There's no admission charge, but it's customary to reward the helpful attendants at the end of your visit. Hours are limited during the current restoration, so check first.

Across the street is the church of **Vittore e Carlo,** also by Bianco. Two facing stairways form the entrace to the higher-than-street-level church. Behind the altar, the *Madonna of Fortune,* carved in wood, was once the figurehead of an Irish ship.

Two more Bianco palaces on Via Balbi—dell'Università (No. 5) and Durazzo Pallavicini (No. 1)—bring us to the Piazza della Nunziata. The **church of the Annunciation** off to the left is one of Genoa's most interesting baroque churches. Though badly damaged during World War II, you can still see its spectacular ceiling frescoes and several paintings by Genoan Bernardo Strozzi.

Pass through Via Cairoli to much admired Via Garibaldi, a great innovation in urban architecture in the 16th century. The placement and form of the buildings were planned as a unit. Art lovers will want to stop at No. 11, the **Palazzo Bianco** (White Palace), so named because of the original colour of its walls. This museum provides a good introduction to Ligurian art, and its Flemish and Dutch collections are also

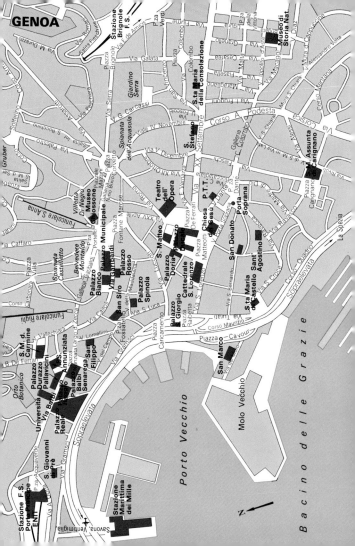

notable. See especially the paintings by Anthony Van Dyck and by Strozzi.

At No. 18, Via Garibaldi, the baroque **Palazzo Rosso** (Red Palace) contains many paintings of the Genoese school, as well as such masters as Titian, Veronese, Caravaggio, more Van Dyck and Rubens. There are also collections of wood carvings by Antonio Maragliano, an artist whose work you'll encounter all along the Riviera, and pottery from Savona, formerly the great ceramic centre of Liguria.

Make a small detour to another art gallery, the **Palazzo Spinola,** in the old town's Piazza di Pellicceria (Square of the Furriers). The palace was originally built in the 16th century for the Grimaldi family. The Spinolas bought it, enlarged it and increased its art treasures. They were patrons of Van Dyck during his stay in Genoa and the palace contains many examples of his work. Note the portrait of a child taken from a larger work—it's rumoured that the canvas was cut when Van Dyck ran away with his sitter, the patron's wife. Now headquarters of the National Gallery of Liguria, the palace is open without charge. Ring the bell to gain admittance.

To tour Genoa's other major sights, begin at Piazza Corvetto with its statues of Victor Emmanuel II and Mazzini. Inside the adjacent park is the **Museo Chiossone,** a remarkable collection of oriental art, gathered by an Italian official who spent 30 years in Tokyo. It will appeal to anyone, even those with no special knowledge of Japanese art.

Down Via Roma, you reach Genoa's main square, Piazza De Ferrari dominated by its central fountain and the tall, gaunt façade of the Palazzo Ducale, now the Courts of Justice. The present structure is the result of 16th- and 17th-century additions to the 13th-century town hall. Through the open doorways you can see statues of Andrea Doria (by Montorsoli) and Giovanni Andrea Doria (by Carlone), both mutilated in an uprising in 1787.

Piazza San Matteo, behind the ducal palace, is a small, quiet square that has remained more or less intact from the Middle Ages. Handsome mansions built by the Dorias surround San Matteo, the Doria family church.

In the church del Gesù (or SS. Ambrogio e Andrea) just off Piazza de Ferrari, you'll find a sculptured group, *Il Pre-*

sepio by Carlone, *The Ascension* by Guido Reni and two paintings by Rubens, *St. Ignatius Curing a Mad Woman* and *The Circumcision*.

It's claimed that Genoa's cathedral of **San Lorenzo** was in use as early as the 9th century. Incorporated in the outer right wall are fragments of Roman ornaments and remains of 3rd- and 4th-century A.D. sarcophagi. In any case, it was rebuilt and redone numerous times and the result is a harmonious blend of styles—including Romanesque, Gothic and Renaissance. An excellent publication, available in various languages, identifies the many paintings and carvings decorating the cathedral. Be sure to visit the **Tesoro** (Treasury), off to the left near the Cibo chapel. Among its prized possessions: the *Sacro Catino* a green-glass chalice supposedly used by Christ at the Last Supper.

In Piazza Dante, you'll see a small house, incongruous

Art in Genoa
Somehow, the painters of Genoa missed out on the Renaissance. While Florence and Pisa were swept away by enthusiasm for classical ideals, Genoa continued to build Goth-

ic churches. Her commercial links with the north influenced her artistic inclinations. Niçois Lodovico BREA (1450–1523) perpetuated the Gothic tradition in painting and attracted many followers in Liguria.

In the 16th century, Luca CAMBIASO (1527–85) brought new life to the local art scene. The most important Genoan painter of his time, his frescoes decorate many of the city's palaces and show clearly the influence of Correggio and the Venetians.

Bernardo STROZZI (1581–1664) started out as a mannerist and ended in full baroque splendour. The work of Rubens (who visited Genoa in 1607) made a deep impression on him—which you can see in Strozzi's intense colours and sweeping strokes. Rubens kept in touch after returning home and later sent an altarpiece for the church del Gesù.

Another Fleming who left his mark here was Anthony VAN DYCK, the darling of the Genoese nobility. During Van Dyck's stay (1621–27), the patricians vied for the privilege of sitting for the great portrait artist.

All over Liguria you'll see the work of Antonio Maria MARAGLIANO (1644–1739). His lovely wooden, polychrome statues adorn both village and city churches.

among towering buildings. A marble plaque announces it as the reconstructed home of Christopher Columbus's father, where the explorer is said to have spent his youth. But the most imposing landmark on the square—and one historically much more certain—is the **Porta Soprana,** twin towers

Great lion sits patiently by San Lorenzo's French Gothic façade.

which formed part of the walls built to defend the city in the 12th century.

Out of Piazza De Ferrari runs impressive Via XX Settembre which unites Genoa's old town with its new. Along this broad avenue, you'll find elegant shops beneath covered archways, flanked by magni-

ficent palaces of the grand epoch of the end of the 19th century.

The XX Settembre spills into Piazza della Vittoria (Victory Square), with its arch commemorating those who died in World War I. Overlooking the square is a grass mound bearing cut-outs of the three anchors and boats of Columbus.

For a splendid view of the whole of Genoa, take the funicular to **Monte Righi.** It leaves from the Largo della Zecca (between Via Balbi and Via Garibaldi).

Niccolò Paganini

The "diabolical" violinist was a star long before the media invented stardom. Born in Genoa in 1782, Paganini the child prodigy gave his first concert, performing his own compositions, at the age of 12. His fame grew constantly, as did his reputation for loose living and gambling. Paganini's tours were so popular that tickets cost up to five times the normal price. Finally his debauchery—and the envy of less talented contemporaries—caught up with him.

Paganini died in 1840. His tomb is in Parma, but his legendary violin, a 1742 Guarnerio del Gesù, is proudly displayed in Genoa in the Palazzo Municipale.

27

Riviera di Ponente

Genoa to Ventimiglia

Along the hundred miles of coastline curving gradually southwestwards from Genoa to the French border, you'll find a variety of sightseeing surprises as well as all kinds of holiday facilities. Buses and trains run regularly along this western Riviera, but unless you have a yacht or power boat, exploring is best by car.

Not much of a resort now, PEGLI (10 km. to the west) used to be known as "the beach of Genoa". The town does boast several handsome mansions from grander days and two interesting museums—one maritime, with a collection of maps, globes and ship models (in the Villa Doria); the other containing archaeological discoveries from the area (in the Villa Pallavicini, set in a luxuriant park).

Genoa's dockyard and industrial sprawl continues for some way, but at ARENZANO, about 22 kilometres along the seaside Via Aurelia, the influence of the city finally fades. Surrounded by mountains, balmy Arenzano offers a large, wide beach, an outdoor swimming pool, sailing boats to rent and other sports facilities including golf, tennis and riding. It's possible to rent a hillside villa or flat set among the pine trees.

A few kilometres further on at COGOLETO, you'll find an ideal spot for a quiet holiday. A former fishing village with

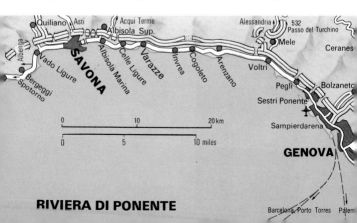

RIVIERA DI PONENTE

narrow streets and brightly painted houses, Cogoleto is a charming little resort. It has a fine beach and excellent camping installations.

Varazze, the first major resort of Savona province (34 km. from Genoa) is set in a bowl of green hills, with a long promenade along a broad sandy beach. Columns of tall palm trees and a profusion of flowers delight the eye. Despite its large modern yacht harbour and new buildings, the town has preserved much of its old-world atmosphere. In the north corner of the old walls, you'll find the 10th-century façade of the original church of Sant' Ambrogio. The present church, built in 1535, has a 13th-century campanile. Inside are works by local artists Maragliano, de Maestri and Cambiaso. A few minutes down Via Aurelia at PIANI D'INVREA is a residential village with a beach and swimming pool.

After passing through CELLE LIGURE, once a fashionable resort now cut in two by the coastal highway, you come to **Albisola** (43 km. from Genoa) founded by the Romans as a health spa. Today it enjoys a measure of international fame for something entirely different—as a centre of ceramic art. This resort is actually two contiguous villages, Albisola Superiore and Albisola Marina, sharing a long beach with a seaside swimming pool.

About 300 years ago ceramists from Savona, then the leading centre for the craft, moved to Albisola where a unique white and red clay is quarried. Prize pieces are displayed at a ceramics museum. Noted local artists include Tullio d'Albisola, Agenore Fabbri, Aligi Sassu and Angelo Barile. Visit any of the factories: you'll see potters and painters working side by side, realizing their own conceptions or decorating the finished articles.

The San Nicolò parish church in Albisola Superiore dates back to 1067; the church of Nostra Signora della Neve with its imposing dome is also worth visiting. The Villa Gavotti, a perfect example of the baroque residence built for the della Rovere family, holds an international music festival in August. In Albisola Marina, take a stroll along the Lungomare degli Artisti, a seaside promenade paved with mosaics, and see the church of Nostra Signora della Concordia with its altarpiece of 48 polychrome enamelled tiles made in 1576.

SAVONA (54 km. from Ge- **29**

Ligurian art from different ages —the Romanesque church of Noli and a 20th-century ceramacist.

noa), known as Savo in Roman times, is primarily a port and industrial centre. Long a rival of Genoa, it was finally taken over in 1528. The Genoese fort from that era can be seen incorporated now into a steel works off Via Aurelia. In the 19th century the fort held two famous prisoners: Pope Pius VII (1809–12) and Mazzini (1830–31). Confined to quarters by Napoleon, the pope showed his defiance by blessing crowds from the balcony *(Loggetta Papale)*.

Via Paleocapa, the arcaded central artery of this provincial capital, leads to the Leon Pancaldo tower which honours a local seaman who served as Magellan's navigator on the first round-the-world voyage in 1520. Savona's cathedral, beautifully set among trees, was

built in the late 16th century to replace a medieval forerunner, though the present façade was added in 1886. The richly decorated interior contains a 12th-century baptismal font, 15th-century choir stalls and a triptych by Lodovico Brea.

In a former palace on Via Quarda Superiore is the **Pinacoteca Civica.** The steep steps inside the vaulted rooms of the gallery will lead you through an exquisite collection of paintings and ceramics. Look for Gioacchino Assereto's *Cristo alla Colonna* and his intensely dramatic *Sacrifice of Isaac* (17th century). Tucked into a corner in the fourth gallery is a beautiful *Madonna and Child and St. John* by Luca Cambiaso. Ceramics from the 16th and 17th centuries show the Savona school at its height.

The first centre north of Savona, VADO LIGURE, was an important Roman military base. The Civic Museum con- **31** tains relics of that period. Two of six Roman bridges built here in the 2nd century B.C. are still in good condition. The San Giacomo fortress (1500) and the lighthouse on the seafront are worth a visit. With a wide sandy shore and flat hinterland, Vado Ligure was chosen as a possible landing site by the Allies during World War II. In fact, they went to the beaches of Saint-Tropez.

The hillside hamlet of Bergeggi faces out to a small island of the same name. Apart from remains of a cylindrical Roman tower and the ruins of a monastery built by monks from Provence in 992, the islet is a paradise for scuba divers. On the mainland you can visit the Bergeggi grottoes. One, called the "Grotto of Love", contains a lake, stalactites and stalagmites. The Capo del Maiolo promontory is supposed to be the site of a castle where those legendary, tragic lovers, Heloise and Abelard, once stayed.

SPOTORNO (60 km. from Genoa) offers sailing, waterskiing and an underwater diving school, plus an art festival. In the parish church of Santissima Annunziata, see several works by Genoan Antonio Maragliano and, in the oratory, votive offerings of sailors— sailing ships in bottles. The Spotorno area is noted for its apricots.

Three kilometres away, the turreted medieval village of **Noli** was for centuries the bitter enemy of Spotorno. You'll see part of its old walls, a few of the 72 original towers, and

arches and portals of green stone. Fishermen still ply their ancient trade on the sandy beach, which has a promenade of palm trees and the usual facilities for tourists. In mid-August, a pageant at Castello di Monte Ursino commemorates a pirate attack of 1,000 years ago. Of special interest is the restored 11th-century church of **San Paragorio,** one of the best examples of pure Romanesque style in Italy.

The Malpasso promontory separates Noli from Varigotti, a holiday centre with two quite separate styles. Emerging from the highway tunnel you'll see the old quarter with flat-roofed beachside houses in Mediterranean style, tiny gardens and squares. The narrow lanes here used to be blocked by iron gates against pirates: the tiny bay was known as the Bay of the Saracens and the beach is said to have been a favourite landing place for the pirate "Redbeard". Ruins of a watch-tower, from which guns fired down on the raiders, can be found atop the promontory. In contrast, modern Varigotti has a promenade along the shore, flanked by apartment houses and tourist villas. All holiday facilities are available, including excellent bathing establishments on the wide sandy beach.

Finale Ligure (72 km. from Genoa), in fact, not one, but four resorts, also played an important role in Ligurian history. While many Riviera towns surrendered their independence to the Genoese in the 14th century, Finale re-

RIVIERA DI PONENTE

sisted. It was governed by the Marquis of Savona, who, caught up in struggles between Genoa and Milan, appealed to Spain for help. Finale thus became a bridgehead for the Spanish empire in Italy, thereby expanding its maritime activities. After the decline of Spain, the Genoese ruled Finale from 1713 until 1796. In 1815, following a spell under Napoleonic control, it passed to the Kingdom of Sardinia.

The best view of this hilly part of the coastline is from FINALBORGO or from the 15th-century Gavone castle on the heights above. Not far off, you'll find the medieval basilica of San Biagio which has a rich treasury and an elegant, eight-sided Gothic bell-tower.

Descending to FINALE MARINA, wander around the old town before visiting the large baroque church of San Giovanni Battista. Note the 15th-century slate portal of Palazzo Lavega nearby. The vineyards here produce a delicate white wine, Lamassina.

Scores of deep caves honeycomb the mountainous Finale area between Capo Noli and Capo Caprazoppa. In days of yore, prehistoric man inhabited some of them. Possibly the best to visit is the Valdemino grotto west of Finale Marina. For in-

formation about the caves, see the local tourist office.

Below the Caprazoppa mountain shoulder nestles another old town expanded into a modern holiday centre— PIETRA LIGURE. Known for centuries for construction of boats, it still has its *cantiere navale* (shipyard). The sprawling town

Back up in the hills, Martinetto with its Napoleonic fortresses.

also possesses a long promenade, much of it shaded by closely planted palm trees, and a sandy beach with the usual water sports and many cafés. The 18th-century parish church of San Nicola di Bari in a delightful square contains dark wooden choir stalls from the cathedral of Marseilles. Like so many Italian churches, it fills to capacity at Sunday evening mass.

Once the feudal domain of the illustrious Doria family, LOANO (82 km. from Genoa) **35**

today is a pleasantly unassuming spot. In its old town by the banks of the Nimbalto river you can stroll along picturesque, narrow streets dating back six centuries. The austere town hall, formerly a Doria palace, has a geometric-figured mosaic floor from a 3rd-century Roman villa. The long, wide sand-and-shingle beach accommodates just a few modest rows of beach chairs and bathing huts and, in a piazza just off Via Aurelia, a lively market offers all kinds of cheeses, fruit, vegetables and flowers every Friday morning. There are also many charming walks into the foothills behind Loano.

A short distance separates Loano from BORGHETTO SANTO SPIRITO with its pleasant little square and sandy beach. A centre for fruit, vegetables and pickled fish kept in earthenware pots, Borghetto is better known as the starting point for a visit to the **Caves of Toirano** —a memorable experience.

In 1890 a group of scientists entered the primary cave and found the remains of tribes who had lived there from time immemorial. But the discoveries

Caves of Toirano—stalagmites, stalactites and prehistoric bones.

were not considered of particular importance since many such existed in the mountains. In 1944 the caves were used as shelter against wartime bombing. Six years later, remembering bats and a draught of air which had escaped from a fissure, local volunteers took the risk of exploring further. Eventually they discovered enormous underground caverns and corridors carved out of the rocks by flowing water, with countless stalactites and stalagmites of rose, green and white. They also found a quantity of bones of large prehistoric bears. These animals probably came into the subterranean passages by an entrance that was later blocked (but now reopened) and died there. More dramatic still was a footprint engraved in the stone, which modern scientific investigation proved to be of a Neanderthal man from 30,000 years ago.

The caves are open every morning and afternoon; you may well be guided around the underground wonders by the man who made the discoveries.

Continuing on Via Aurelia, you go through a tunnel and emerge at the modern resort area of CERIALE with numerous apartment blocks and hotels for winter and summer tourism. Leaving Ceriale by the road

parallel with the sea, you'll pass impressive market gardens which lie cheek by jowl with camping and caravan sites.

After the gardens comes the fascinating old town of **Albenga** (89 km. from Genoa), once a Roman port but now almost a mile from the sea because of the shifting of the Centa river in the 13th century.

The Romans shipped out oil, wine and grain; today Albenga is noted for year-round production of fresh vegetables, especially artichokes which are often grown beneath glass and flown out of nearby Villanova airport daily to the markets of Europe. The fertile soil of this alluvial plain yields as many as ten crops a year.

Once the capital of the Ingauni Ligurians, Albenga was conquered in 181 A.D. by the Romans who turned it into a lively port. The town's old quarter is confined within a small area north of Piazza del Popolo. Here the streets are narrow and twisting, often passing beneath low arches. Through open doorways you'll see artisans repairing and restoring furniture, bottling wine, crafting shoes and leather goods.

Signalling the pride of Albenga, three red brick towers soar skywards at Piazza San

Michele and Piazza IV Novembre, the medieval heart of town. The 11th-century cathedral of San Michele was rebuilt in 1300 and is now being restored. Take a look at the decorated ceiling, simple altar and remains of early frescoes. The adjacent **baptistery,** a rare example of Paleo-Christian architecture, dates back to the 5th century. Now part of the Museo Ingauno, it's open mornings and afternoons. The octagonal interior contains the baptistery's original granite pillars from Corsica and an alcove decorated in a curiously Byzantine-Oriental mosaic. There are several Roman amphorae,

which were used in the construction of the cupola, and tombs in the wall alcoves.

In the nearby Roman Naval Museum located in the Palazzo Peloso-Cepolla, you'll learn how skillful the Romans were at constructing and loading ships. On display are timbers from 100 B.C. and more than a hundred ancient amphorae found in the sea off Albenga.

From Albenga, those with a car and a head for mountain heights can make an interesting trip away from the Riviera's beachside bustle. Take the state road signposted Garessio-Ceva to LECA (3 km.) with its 14th-century bell-tower and even earlier Saracen tower. Once across the *autostrada* continue alongside the river to the old fortified borough of CISANO SUL NEVA. Passing through abundant fruit orchards you start to climb until MARTINETTO, where there's the first of a chain of four Napoleonic fortresses which guarded this end of the Albenga plain.

Shortly thereafter you reach the medieval village of **Zuccarello,** standing next to a rushing stream with a lovely Romanesque bridge. Inside, the streets are narrow and the arcades are lined with shops and dark passageways. Stone stairways climb around corners, plants grow undisturbed from the walls of tiny houses. The atmosphere is friendly and totally tranquil, a world apart from the seashore down below.

Hard work and laughter have both left their mark on Ligurian faces. **39**

If you decide to tarry, the bread, wine, olives and local salami are delicious. Spending half a day in this untouched haven cannot be too highly recommended.

After Zuccarello, the road climbs more quickly. Then you swing to the right just before the village of ERLI, up a precipitous winding route with wonderful panoramic views of the heights of Piedmont and Albenga plain. The fascinating town of **Castelvecchio di Rocca Barbena** is a maze of tiny, steep streets where animals are kept in groundfloor stables of the houses. Tortuous winding paths and stairs lead up eventually to a 13th-century castle, now being restored.

On your return it's worth making a small detour off to the left to visit **Villanova d'Albenga,** an ancient fortress with walls and towers still intact. Once through the portal you'll see the 12th-century church of Santo Stefano and Santa Maria della Rotonda of 1520.

Back along the coast, **Alassio** (96 km. from Genoa) is one of Italy's most popular holiday centres. This former feudal town which belonged to the monks of nearby Isola Gallinara now contains over 200 hotels. Each year sees international fishing contests, sailing regattas and the Festival of Muretto in August, featuring a beauty competition. The town's *muretto* (little wall) has hundreds of ceramic tiles reproducing the signatures of famous visitors such as Winston Churchill, Ernest Hemingway and Sophia Loren. Alassio's busy morning market sells clothing, fruit and vegetables,

but above all flowers and cheeses from inland. The deep harbour can handle the largest yacht, with ample mooring along an inside breakwater wall, a floating pontoon and a fixed wharf. East of the main town another harbour has snack bars and restaurants where one can relax watching people tinker with their boats, a most amiable pursuit. For

The long sandy beach of Alassio before the arrival of midday crowds.

serious sightseeing, try the Sant' Ambrogio church. Built in the 11th century and restored in the 16th, it has paintings inside by Giovanni De Ferrari (1598–1669) and a polychrome group by the ubiquitous Maragliano. The palace of Scofferi is also worth a visit, if only to admire the *Crucifix* attributed to Giambologna.

A Blooming Business

It all started in the 1850s when a French journalist came to Nice (then Italian) and opened up a flowershop. He had the bright idea of sending flowers back to Paris in boxes. Another floral pioneer, Ludwig Winter, was a German landscape architect. He planned the elaborate Hanbury Gardens near Ventimiglia (see p. 55) and set up a horticultural business. Winter was the first to show that flowers could be cultivated for profit.

Others followed on a larger scale—like the Acquasciati brothers of San Remo, who planted 5,000 rose bushes. And flower growing became an industry. About 70 per cent of those involved in agriculture today raise flowers. Of course, the steep slopes of the area present real problems. But with perseverance and ingenuity, the Ligurians have succeeded in making the most difficult land bloom.

At LAIGUEGLIA you can watch the comings and goings of a small fishing fleet while relaxing on the long sandy beach. Life here centres around the ancient bastion and the winding *carugi,* a shopping area under cool archways. Another attraction is the baroque twin-towered church of San Matteo, whose dimly lit interior contains works by Maragliano, De Ferrari and Bernardo Strozzi. At night Laigueglia offers both discotheques and dancing at posh seaside terraces.

MARINA DI ANDORA, last of the coastal resort towns in Savona province, has a wealth of holiday apartments, a few hotels and pensions, a harbour for small shallow-draught boats and a sand-shingle beach. Stylish villas perch among trees on the mountainside. Following signs for *castello* in the hills behind Andora, you'll find the beautiful, simple church of **San Giacomo e San Filippo** (13th century), whose unadorned stone of light ochre seems to glow.

The small hillside village of **Cervo** (108 km. from Genoa), with its red roofs, steep steps,

Delightful Cervo, banned to cars, is mostly medieval and unspoiled.

archways and alleyways, is wholly delightful. Founded more than ten centuries ago, it remains mostly medieval in feeling. Unspoiled, but hardly unknown: every year in July and August crowds throng into the town for an international chamber-music festival. It's held in a picturesque square in front of the ornate baroque church of San Giovanni Battista, which commands a fine panorama of the scenic coastline. Inside, look particularly for Maragliano's group, *The Family of St. John,* and for a carved *Christ on the Cross.*

Cervo's beach, mixed shingle and sand, is approached through railway arches; it has many bathing huts, moorings for small boats and rocky projections into the water that are favoured by landbound fishermen.

Stretched along a flat coastline above a long extended beach, SAN BARTOLOMEO AL MARE is well endowed with vacation apartments and camping sites. A breakwater parallel with the beach makes paddling particularly safe for children.

Straw-hatted steed steers tourists around streets of Diano Marina.

The shaded promenade bordering the sea is almost a mile long. In the 13th-century parish church, look for the splendid polyptych on wooden panels (1562) of the school of Lodovico Brea.

Recent archaeological finds prove that **Diano Marina,** the next resort along the coast, has been inhabited since the Stone Age. In the wooded hills overlooking the village stood a sacred temple to the ancient Ligurian god of the hunt. In Roman times he became assimilated with the goddess Diana, hence the name of the town. From such distant beginnings, the modern well-equipped resort of Diano Marina has grown. You can make a number of agreeable walks through lush countryside where olive groves and sub-tropical shrubs thrive. Orange trees line the town's avenues; and you'll see agave and padded prickly pear everywhere. On Corpus Christi day the main streets are carpeted with flower petals arranged in delicate patterns, and on the night of Ferragosto (August 15), fireworks and lights floating on the sea make a beautiful spectacle.

After passing attractive Capo Berta you reach **Imperia** (120 km. from Genoa), the provincial capital, which also considers itself the main town of the "Riviera dei Fiori" between Alassio and the French border. Many other spots along this delightful—and truly floriferous—coast would no doubt dispute that title, but they can't challenge Imperia's claim as the regional centre for olive oil and pasta production.* Many people also know the town for its international chess festival, held each September.

Imperia is a "new" town, formed in 1923 by the union of Oneglia and Porto Maurizio. Excellent breakwaters provide sheltered harbours and beaches along the curving shoreline. Porto Maurizio's old town, known as Il Parrasio, is enclosed by Corso Garibaldi and Via Felice Cascione. Stairways and narrow alleys climb to Piazza del Duomo and the basilica of San Maurizio. While you're there, take a look at the medieval church of San Pietro. Oneglia claims fame as the birthplace (in 1466) of Admiral Andrea Doria, "saviour" of Genoa (see p. 17).

From Porto Maurizio (Via Felice Cascione) and Oneglia (Via XX Aprile), you can take various bus or car trips inland towards the heights of Piedmont. Strongly recommended are **Montegrazie** for the 15th-century Sanctuary of the Madonna, with its wonderfully worked stone construction and inspiring frescoes, **Pieve di Teco,** known for its handicrafts, **Colle di Nava,** where they make lavander water and perfume,

---

* For an appetizing insight into spaghetti and such, visit the museum devoted to this hallowed subject outside of town (see also p. 97).

46

and the winter ski resort of **Monesi.**

Next along Via Aurelia two little seaside resorts, SANTO STEFANO AL MARE and RIVA LIGURE, succeed one another. Both are friendly places of some charm, not yet built up to the proportion of the larger Riviera holiday centres.

Many bathing establishments line the wide beach at ARMA DI TAGGIA, where a semi-skyscraper block is an unusual feature of the long shoreline promenade. Arma di Taggia

Steep steps and alleys lead up to the old town of Porto Maurizio.

forms a single commune with TAGGIA, 3 kilometres inland, an ancient town set in a valley noted for its violets and fruit groves. In Taggia, visit the restored 11th-century church of the Madonna del Canneto and the San Domenico monastery of the Dominican friars (ring the bell for admittance). The cloister, built in the 1400s, is a peaceful haven with an arched inner court. Look for the works by Lodovico Brea from Nice in the adjacent church.

An interesting inland trip from Arma di Taggia takes you through CASTELLARO, with its views down to the sea, to the Sanctuary of Lampedusa poised on top of a wooded hill with a wonderful panorama of the whole coastline.

Another sanctuary, Sacro Cuore, was built at the end of the 19th century at BUSSANA on the coast to commemorate the 1887 earthquake that destroyed much of nearby Bussana Vecchia. It is a richly decorated, baroque-style church, with a wealth of privately donated works by artists from all over Italy. Make sure to see the wooden choir stalls

Long deserted, Bussana Vecchia is coming back as an artists' centre.

representing episodes of the New Testament by Cesare Zonca of Bergamo and the sensitive frescoes over the nave by Raffaello Resio. Some houses still stand among the hills at BUSSANA VECCHIA, roofless, forlorn, abandoned by terror-stricken people. But life is coming back; one by one the ruined hulks are being repaired. Not in the conventional way, but by artists who, among the rubble and broken beams, are creating studios and galleries for their own highly individual works.

San Remo (144 km. from Genoa), Liguria's glittering and cosmopolitan resort, likes to think it's the first with the most. And so, for generations of people on holiday, it has been. San Remo's marvellous year-round climate (more annual sunshine than anywhere else on the Riviera, you'll hear), its ideal hillside position on the sea, its overwhelming profusion of flowers (the world's "busiest flower market", they say), brought it to prominence long ago as a winter resort for the rich. After World War I, noblemen fleeing the Bolsheviks in Russia sought it out and built large, if only sometimes elegant, villas. The Russian church near stately Corso Imperatrice recalls that era. A **49**

casino was erected and extravagant hotels offered impeccable service in the "grand manner". But the "grand manner" was one of the first casualties of World War II. In the impecunious peace that followed, San Remo had to adjust to a more modest class of tourists. Some high-flying customers still show up, but at the oncesnooty casino gaming has given

Gone are the days of Russian royalty, but San Remo wears its glamorous past with grace and now plays host to wide range of visitors.

way to gambling, and ties are no longer required.

The huge yacht harbour here offers facilities for pleasure boats of all sizes. There's a wide beach area to the east and if you've any spare energy, tennis, golf or riding are all available. If not, you can stroll along a promenade of coloured criss-cross tiles beneath palm trees, alongside green and yellow agaves.

"Special events" follow each other through San Remo's year —a song festival, men's fashion festival, Milan–San Remo bicycle race, regatta. In season, an orchestra performs nightly and on Sunday afternoons. Go

early in the morning to the **flower market** off Piazza Colombo, the central square at the start of Corso Garibaldi: what a heady sight and smell it provides, with tightly budded roses, carnations, the elaborate and exotic sharing stall space with the gentle and familiar. Wander the narrow rampways and alleys of San Remo's colourful old town (known as La Pigna), up to the sanctuary of the Madonna della Costa with a *Mother and Child* (c. 1400) by Nicolò da Voltri above the main altar.

To get above and away from it all, take the cable car from Corso degli Inglesi all the way up to MONTE BIGNONE (4,200 ft.) for fine panoramic views. The ride, with intermediate stops at the golf course and the pine-woods resort of SAN ROMOLO, takes about 45 minutes.

A strongly recommended trip from San Remo is to **Coldirodi,** centre of rose cultivation. There you can tour the admirable Rambaldi Biblioteca e Pinacoteca, containing old manuscripts, a stamp collection and a fine arts gallery. Ring for admittance (from 3

Giardini Hanbury—the ultimate garden—not far from Ventimiglia. **53** to 5 p.m.) and a curator will show you around.

OSPEDALETTI luxuriates in its flowers, palm trees and eucalyptus with promenades and bathing establishments along a sandy beach. Its name may come from the Latin word for hospitality—or from a hospital *(ospedale)* founded here, they say, by the Knights of Rhodes. Corso Marconi and Via Cavour offer splendid views over this "refined and elegant" town, as it justifiably styles itself.

Bordighera, "Town of the Palms", each year proundly sends the Vatican artistically entwined *palmorelli* (young shoots from palm trees). The privilege dates to a legendary near-accident in 1586 when the huge Egyptian obelisk in St. Peter's Square was being laboriously erected. The pope, Sixtus V, decreed silence, threatening death for anyone who broke it. The ropes holding the obelisk were about to give when one man, risking all, shouted "wet the ropes"! They did; the day was saved. The pope forgave him and granted one request: "My hometown of Bordighera grows the most wonderful palms, Your Holiness. My wish is that we be permitted to supply the Vatican during Holy Week!"

According to tradition, the first palm was brought here from Egypt by Sant'Ampelio. This 4th-century holy man supposedly spent the rest of his life in a grotto located at the end of Lungomare Argentina. A church named in his honour has been built over it.

In the old section of town, the Bordighetta, you'll find arcades with vaulted arches and the parish church of Santa Maria Maddelena. The railway separates much of Bordighera from the beaches, which you get to by numerous archways. Apart from its long-standing reputation as a holiday resort, Bordighera likes to think of itself as the centre of humour: each year, in fact, it holds an international humour festival. On the serious side, the Institute for Ligurian Studies is here, too, with an exhibition on anthropology of the early Ligurians.

Ventimiglia (162 km. from Genoa), last point-of-call before the French border, has been the scene of struggles since the Romans conquered it and bestowed the name Albintimilium. You can visit the excavated Roman ruins, including an amphitheatre, in the Nervia section. Most of the archaeological artefacts are now on view in the Civico Museo. In Ventimiglia's medieval old town see the 11th-12th-century **cathedral** with its Gothic portal and adjacent baptistery of the same period. Nearby, the Romanesque church of San Michele contains the original 11th-century crypt with marble columns and milestones (see the custodian at 16, Via Garibaldi, for admittance to the baptistery and San Michele). Take a moment, too, to enjoy the splendid view from the old town.

Most visitors will want to see the **Hanbury Gardens** on the slopes of CAPO MORTOLA, 7 kilometres west of Ventimiglia. Sir Thomas Hanbury bought the property with its old castle in 1862 and created a remarkable botanical preserve with more than 3,000 varieties of plants and trees.

A final visit, not inappropriately, to where it all began: the caves of the **Balzi Rossi** near the frontier. In this important palaeontological site, patient archaeologists have uncovered evidence of primitive Mediterranean man. You can inspect several grottoes that were inhabited in Paleolithic times (at Ponte San Ludovico right on the French-Italian border line) and also visit the Museum of Prehistory to see the remains of Cro-Magnon man, his primitive weapons and cooking utensils beside him.

Monaco

Renowned for its glamour, the Principality of Monaco* perches on the French Riviera just a short distance from the Italian border. On the 453 hilly acres comprising this independent state live 23,500 inhabitants, though only 4,500 are native-born Monegasques. Their currency is French francs; their language, mostly French. Italian and English are widely understood. You'd be unlucky to have bad weather on a visit: Monaco boasts more than 2,500 hours of sunshine a year.

Four areas make up the pocket-sized principality: Monaco, the old town on a rocky promontory with the seat of government and palace of the Grimaldi family, who have ruled almost uninterruptedly since 1297; Monte Carlo, the sophisticated holiday resort with its famed gambling casino; La Condamine, the harbour with berthings for the largest yachts; and Fontvieille, reclaimed from the sea for an ultra-modern development under construction. Everywhere there are parks and flowers. You'll find the Street of Agaves,

---

* Berlitz also publishes a guide to the FRENCH RIVIERA with a section on Monaco.

the Avenue of Lemons, the Steps of the Flowers, the streets of Geraniums, Iris, Lilacs, Oranges, Roses and Violets.

Touring this realm of His Serene Highness Prince Rainier III, who acceded in 1949, you'll want to climb the steps of the medieval Rampe Major to see the colourful changing of the guard at the Place du Palais. It takes place just before noon every day. Part of the **palace's** left wing contains a museum with a collection of Napoleonic memorabilia and the principality's archives, coins and stamps (open daily except Monday).

Below the Jardins Saint-Martin is the vast **Oceanographic Museum** and **Aquarium,** directed by underwater explorer Jacques Cousteau.

From the station, a steep walk or bus ride will take you to the Jardin Exotique, open all year, which features plants from everywhere, a grotto and a Museum of Prehistoric Anthropology with dinosaurs and pterodactyls.

At the new **National Museum** you'll find the life work of Madeleine de Galéa—a fascinating collection of old dolls, automatons and miniature items. The museum is north of Avenue Princesse Grace in the Villa Sauber whose gardens contain more than a thousand rose trees.

Monte Carlo owes much of its prosperity to the Société des Bains de Mer, a club with facilities for "sea bathing and visitors" founded in 1861. Its casino inspired a popular song, "The Man Who Broke the Bank at Monte Carlo", and you'll see many trying to emulate him in the opulently decorated gaming rooms.

Throughout the year the principality stages extravagant spectacles, gala evenings and concerts. Once the reserve of the very wealthy, it now manages to cater for all types of people on holiday without losing any of its tone. Hotels, pensions and restaurants are often less expensive than one would expect. Monaco's good taxi service is known for its courteous drivers and scrupulously clean vehicles.

From Italy you can reach Monaco on the A10 *autostrada* (Genoa–Ventimiglia–Monaco) or the Via Aurelia. Frequent trains run from Genoa to Nice, which may involve a change at Ventimiglia.

Monegasques catch up on the day's news in renowned casino capital.

Riviera di Levante

With more strikingly rugged scenery than its sister coastline, the eastern Riviera extends eccentrically for some 66 miles southeast of Genoa. Here, too, you'll have a satisfying choice of sights and holiday resorts, including a few of the most famous in Italy. Trains leave from Genoa's Brignole station; by car you follow the winding Via Aurelia at first, a lesser coastal road further along.

Still part of Genoa's industrial commuter area, QUARTO DEI MILLE is considered a bathing spot by some local inhabitants. The Mille were the 1,000 "Red Shirts" in Garibaldi's historic expedition launched from here (see p. 18).

This coast's first extensive holiday resort is NERVI (11 km. from Genoa), with a stony shingle beach, large public parks and the magnificent mile-and-a-half Anita Garibaldi promenade along the sea, from which cars are banned. Modern art by local painters is displayed at the Villa Serra on Via Capolungo (closed Mondays and Tuesdays), where musical and dramatic performances are also staged. The Villa Luxuro on Via Aurelia has a collection of antiques, arts and crafts, pictures and furniture (open daily except Monday). In summer, Nervi holds a ballet festival.

Sitting side by side, BOGLIASCO and PIEVE LIGURE are two small coastal villages built around steep cliffs. The origins of the church of San Michele above Pieve go back to Roman times.

From here the road dips over

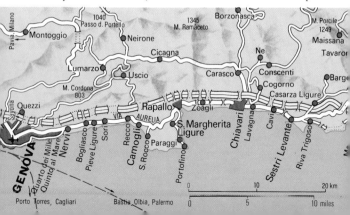

the shelf of a mountain, affording impressive views down to SORI tucked away on a sandy beach. Its parish church, rebuilt in the 17th century, is one of the few that escaped the intensive bombing of this area during World War II. It has a very fine bell-tower.

Nearby RECCO also suffered heavy war-time damage. Now almost completely a town of commuter and holiday apartments, Recco has a wide sand beach from which daily boat excursions leave for San Fruttuoso and go round the point to Portofino.

Up and inland from Recco, where the Genoese Apennines start becoming serious mountains, take a very winding, scenic route up to the summer resorts of USCIO and TORRIGLIA.

Leave Via Aurelia and take the coast road along the promontory of Portofino into **Camogli,** an ancient seaport described by Charles Dickens as "the saltiest, roughest, most piratical little place!" The first glimpse of the town is enchanting—through cypress, poplar and oleander trees you'll see the pocket-sized harbour lined with tall old houses, and a bevy of boats moored on buoys or against an elderly wharf. The houses, painted long ago in bright shades, have faded to a mellow blend of greens and ochres, siennas and whites. The mild, dry climate attracts visitors year-round to this bustling place. You'll find an aquarium, a large swimming pool featuring hotly contested water polo games and a marine museum with many splendid models and

RIVIERA DI LEVANTE

paintings of old sailing vessels. Here, too, is a nautical school founded by the once-famed Captains of Camogli, noted navigators whose descendants can be seen sitting on the harbour walls plaiting and sewing, stitching and knotting elaborate pots for lobster, crab and shrimp. At its height, around 1870, the Camogli sailing fleet numbered about a thousand vessels. The advent of steam and power boats turned the town back into a small fishing port.

At Camogli's 17th-century Santuario del Boschetto, the Mediterranean's worst storms are commemorated each year with votive offerings from sailors and their families. You can also visit the old church of Santa Maria Assunta near the port and, in the picturesque village of **San Fruttuoso** (accessible by boat or foot), the abbey of Capodimonte, where six members of the Doria family are buried.

The second Sunday of May is the occasion of a giant fish fry, Sagra del Pesca, on the quai, with free fish for all.

The road from Camogli through RUTA, with its panoramic view of the Portofino peninsula, turns right and descends into **Santa Margherita Ligure**. This very popular spot caters for both winter and summer visitors. To service the growing flood of yachts and smaller craft, they built an excellent new marina. Strolling the extended front you'll pass many little piazzas with orange trees and the white-flowered *margherita* bush which, in full bloom, can look like a giant snowball. A fish market operates in the mornings at the busy harbour, a colourful general market along Corso Rainusso on Friday mornings. In addition to sailing and waterskiing, you can enroll at the local sub-aqua school to learn diving. Boat excursions leave here for Rapallo and for Portofino. Other boats cross the bay to Sestri Levante.

The richly decorated basilica of Santa Margherita d'Antiochia contains Flemish and Italian paintings and the relics of the saint who gave the town its name. The church of **San Siro** is notable for its astounding gilded and painted ceiling, pink and white pillars and a black and white marble floor. You'll easily spot this church's elegant bell and clock tower, and ochre façade with white

The idyllic harbour of Camogli remains a haven for fishermen.

columns, but its size and unexceptional position on Corso Rainusso give no hint of the visual treasures inside.

South from Santa Margherita Ligure a slender road winds alongside the sea beneath the peninsula's villa-encrusted mountain, passing through PARAGGI, a sleepy collection of

A boat trip around Portofino promontory is worth a bit of a squeeze.

houses in the elbow of a small inlet with the only sand beach in the area.

Portofino comes upon you unexpectedly—you turn a bend in the road, go down a short hill and find yourself in a piazza. From there you must walk. Wisely, both vehicles and new construction have been banned

in the waterfront area. The bay itself, long and narrow and therefore sheltered, provides all-weather mooring for a hundred or more yachts and a wealth of sailing dinghies. It's rimmed by friendly fish restaurants and expensive chic boutiques which preserve the Paris-Rome tone to perfection in style and price. Portofino, you'll notice, is a stop-over for the international jet set, many of whom arrive on those yachts.

Climbing steps cut into rock to the **Castello di San Giorgio,** you'll have an incomparable view of these storied seas and a pleasant promenade. You can take a boat ride round the coast to San Fruttuoso or to other points. There's excellent water-skiing at prices to be negotiated. The parish church contains works by Ligurian artists.

It has been said that Portofino is a paradise many may visit but where few can stay. The apartments and villas, mostly owned by industrialists from Milan, Turin, Genoa and abroad are seldom rented. At the small number of hotels and pensions advance booking is necessary during the season, May to October, and on weekends throughout the year.

The road north from Santa Margherita Ligure joins Via Aurelia outside another cele- **63** brated resort, **Rapallo** (34 km. from Genoa). It's lodged in the depths of the Tigullio gulf, an ideal location with gentle weather that has drawn tourists for centuries. Wealthy British discovered the place after World War I and considered it their exclusive preserve. In the 1950s mass tourism began,

Rapallo's bay offers a wealth of scenery and sporting possibilities.

wealth and class barriers tumbled. Now, of course, Rapallo welcomes all visitors. They enjoy its long promenade and gardens, open-air concerts, an excellent yacht harbour, sailing, water-skiing and scuba-diving facilities. From the dock there are frequent excursions round the coast to Santa Margherita Ligure, Portofino, San Fruttuoso, Punta Chiappa and Camogli.

Rapallo's cathedral was founded between the 5th and 7th centuries by the bishops of Milan; its castle on a pirate-proof rock surrounded by the sea is about a thousand years younger. You'll also see the

arcades and ancient slate portal of the Saline Gate, the only one left in the walls that once enclosed the medieval town.

For a change of pace, try the seven-minute cable-car ride (from Via Castagneto off Via Betti) to the sanctuary of the Madonna di Montallegro for fine views over the harbour and countryside.

Rapallo still basks dimly in its fame as an international meeting site—in 1917 the wartime allies conferred here, in 1920 Italy and Yugoslavia settled their territorial differences with a treaty here, and two years later Russia and Germany signed a friendship pact. Events nowadays are non-political: riding competitions, golf and tennis tournaments, folklore festivals, regattas, clay-pigeon shoots, motor rallies and boxing matches. The local tourist office on Via Diaz has full details.

A short distance along the coast is ZOAGLI, a small village of much charm which would be even nicer without the 70-foot-high railway viaduct spanning the mouth of the bay. Through its arches you'll find excellent swimming facilities and a mole for mooring boats. The shoreline at this mini-resort is jagged; fine walks have been hewn out of the rocks. In the town square you'll admire a beautiful mosaic of black and white pebbles from the sea. For centuries, Zoagli has been famous for its velvet. The secret of their special weaving technique has been passed down from generation to generation.

What immediately strikes the eye at **Chiavari** are the yacht harbour, palm trees, promenade and the railway which runs along the sea front. Though you may have to negotiate a short tunnel to get to the beach, once there the sand stretches away towards the horizon. Chiavari stands at the confluence of five valleys, all populous. The industrial section at the back of town does not intrude on such seaside tourist facilities as an international resort centre with sports for young people, a 150-foot swimming pool, a yacht club and discos and night-clubs.

The cathedral of **Madonna dell'Orto** (Our Lady of the Garden) was built in 1613–33 to commemorate a miraculous image of the Virgin that appeared on a local garden wall. Its fine 50-foot-high entrance

Sestri Levante—the most ordinary street may reveal unexpected art.

portico, *pronao* (1841), is supported by massive pillars of polished marble and carries five bas-reliefs. Among the many art works in the sumptuous interior, Genoan Antonio Maragliano again deserves special attention. You'll find his group carved in wood, representing St. Francis of Assisi, in a niche adjacent to the altar of the Chapel of the Annunciation.

Chiavari and LAVAGNA are contiguous towns separated by the River Entella—and a fierce rivalry! But, along with adjacent CAVI, they offer similar facilities, share the same beach line and sea. On August 14, Lavagna celebrates the day of Torta Fieschi, commemorating an important wedding in the Fieschi family, with a parade and free cake *(torta)*. Lavagna's arches are another reminder of the town's medieval history. So, too, is the **Basilica dei Fieschi** at San Salvatore, 4 kilometres inland (tour buses will take you there). Set in peaceful green hills overlooking the river valley and the sea, the basilica is one of the most important monuments on the Ri-

viera di Levante. It was built between 1245 and 1252 by Pope Innocent IV; the façade is pure Gothic. Inside you can see the cross which the pope wore at the Council of Lyons, when he deposed the Holy Roman Emperor, Frederick II.

Sestri Levante (54 km. from Genoa), considered by many the gem of this part of the coast, straddles a natural isthmus flanked by two bays. At the end of the isthmus is a tree-covered promontory sheltering a yacht harbour. A vast, deep beach with a shallow slope curves around one bay; red-roofed houses of the old town, charmingly painted in pastel colours, border the other. From the promontory's public garden one can climb paths with panoramic views of the sea to the tower where radio inventor Marconi conducted his early experiments. For a memorable sight, go to the Passeggiata dei Cappuccini at sunset.

Sestri's beaches boast all the usual sports, with the scuba-diving reckoned by experts to be particularly good. Fishermen still sail their traditional boats, called *leudi,* from the bay east of the isthmus, but each year the fleet diminishes as young people seek work in tourism or nearby shipyards. Palazzo Rizzi at Via Cappuc-

Levanto's green-and-white church is the scene of local festivities.

cini 10 houses a fine art collection, including work by Caravaggio and Genoese and Venetian artists, plus antique furniture. Apply to the custodian.

After the industrial village of RIVA TRIGOSO, you'll go through some old railway tunnels—long and narrow—which lead somewhat eerily to MONEGLIA. This small and charming resort, surrounded by hills covered with olive trees, has a proud history: two of its galleys took part in the great naval battle of Meloria in 1284 between Genoa and Pisa. A 1290 bas-relief on the church of Santa Croce commemorates this. Inside are beautiful stained-glass windows, and ceiling and wall decorations. Another source of civic pride: the painter Luca Cambiaso was born here in 1527.

The difficulty of getting to Moneglia has kept the tide of mass tourism in check. A small river runs through the town beneath lovely bridges. At the sand and shingle beach are excellent bathing facilities and many sailing boats. You'll also find tennis courts and a football field so close to the sea you need a boat if the ball is kicked out of bounds.

The ruined Monleone and Villafranca castles, both 12th century, mark the limits of Moneglia which itself marks the southern boundary of Genoa province. Ever thin and winding, the coast road then plunges back into old railway tunnels to emerge at DEIVA MARINA, the first resort, geographically, in La Spezia province. This untidily sprawling holiday town has a beach of sand and coloured stones (reds and greens predominate, creating a fantastic effect), and many recently built apartment blocks. A promenade is now being constructed on the bed of the old railway line.

To reach the next village on this coast by car, you'll travel inland on a curving mountain road past the hamlets of Piazza and Castagnola, through Framura and Reggimonti, to join the 332 outside BONASSOLA. The beach here, again of stones and sand, is coloured mauve and turquoise. Tourist facilities, including a hillside bungalow complex, are still modest at Bonassola but prospects are bright since the railway line has been moved from its former position to the back of the village.

Levanto (88 km. from Genoa), gateway to the celebrated Cinque Terre, is a holiday resort in its own right, sitting in the elbow of a bay surrounded by green hills. The promenade with beautiful old villas and gardens, curls around to a jutting promontory. Flowers and palm trees abound. Among the excellent facilities are two campsites, bathing establishments, tennis courts and night-clubs. Preserved in the 13th-14th-century church of Sant'Andrea is a blackened carving of Christ found on a local beach. The church of the Franciscans contains a Strozzi painting, *The Miracle of San Diego*.

A rewarding walk into the hills above Levanto takes you through fields of broom to Monte Rossola (1½ hours); in May and June the hillside is covered in gold. You'll also find lavender and wild thyme, plus magnificent views across the sea to Portofino.

Leaving Levanto by the road through the valley floor and climbing past the hamlets of Ridarolo, Legnaro and Chiesanuova brings one to the road finally being built to open all of the **Cinque Terre** to the motor car. Five historically remote villages make up the Cinque Terre—Monterosso al Mare, Vernazza, Corniglia, Manarola and Riomaggiore. They're simple and starkly beautiful places on a little-visited, rugged fragment of the coast. Pending completion of the road, the best way to reach them all is by a highly unusual train journey through mountain tunnels. Alternatively, there are mule tracks around the steep slopes, or you might arrive by boat.

The five villages are small and unspoiled with some holiday facilities. Vineyards stretch to impossible and, one would think, unworkable heights up mountainsides that frequently look almost vertical. The sweet white wine, *sciacchetrà,* they produce is known even abroad. Five castles stand on peaks above, five fishing harbours on the sea below. Handling boats into and out of the water is a daunting feat of strength and endurance often up slipways carved out of solid rock.

The origins of the hardy people of Cinque Terre are unknown. Some say they are descended from the Etruscans of 2,500 years ago and that they were given shelter in these craggy cliff spaces in return for creating and nurturing the precipitous vineyards. They look shorter than many Italians, often with an Eastern cast to their features, and speak a dialect of their own.

The ancient fishing port of **Monterosso** is the largest of the five, offering good tourist facilities in three small bays. The shore is edged with a salt-and-pepper coloured strand of stones fine enough to be called sandy. Here you can find sailing boats for hire, changing huts and boat trips to the other four villages. A winding street curls around the green-and-white marbled church of San Giovanni Battista. Standing on a headland over a tunnel separating two bays is a bronze statue of St. Francis of Assisi.

Above is the Convento dei Cappuccini, again with the typical local façade of green and white marble. It's well worth climbing the steep path to see the *Crucifixion,* a painting by a follower of Van Dyck, above an altar half way along the left of the nave.

The path to **Vernazza** is no more than a goat track that climbs along terraced vineyards and the sheer face of mountains plunging vertically to the waves. Used for hundreds of years by the inhabitants of Monterosso and Vernazza, it is a strenuous but marvellous two-hour trek past the vines, green and silver-leafed olive orchards and brooks of sparkling water. As you round the last mountain, Vernazza lies before you with its medieval castle seemingly hewn from solid rock. Pastel houses cling to each other. A steep descent through vineyards brings you to

the village, overlooking a well-protected harbour. Quaint alleys lead past shops and rustic restaurants to a fine shingle beach. The houses around the square are pink with green shutters; the fishermen's boats drawn to the top of the slipway form a rainbow. On a rock washed on three sides by the

sea is the church of Santa Margherita d'Antiochia, its style pure Ligurian Gothic.

CORNIGLIA is the only one of the Cinque Terre without a beach. It sits atop a vertically faced cliff from which a winding path descends. Alongside the village wooden bungalows can be rented in summer, with access to a separate shingle beach for bathing.

Continuing past these bungalows along the cliff, a two-hour

Startling sight at Monterosso—stone colossus stares down over the sea.

walk brings one comfortably to MANAROLA, a cluster of red, green, orange and ochre houses, perched on a rock point that seems to hang over the sea. You won't envy the sailors who must somehow negotiate the winding slipway here with their boats. Swimming at this point is strictly the "dive-off-the-rock" variety, though a steep path leads to a shingle beach around the promontory.

Follow the **Via dell'Amore** (Lovers' Lane)—a magnificent 15-minute walk overlooking the sea—to RIOMAGGIORE. Building this town was a miraculous achievement! Huddled around a fissure in the rock, Riomaggiore is deep and narrow with steep, closely packed houses, a mini-piazza and terraces that climb the mountain. A tunnel connects the railway station to the village.

There are few tourist facilities. But while definitely not recommended for the lie-on-the-beach visitor, Riomaggiore has an old charm of its own unlike any other of the Cinque Terre. Buy a glass of local wine from the lady at the outdoor stand, after a stroll through the quiet, car-less alleyways. Retreats like this become ever scarcer.

From Riomaggiore, a good

new road leads across the mountain slopes to LA SPEZIA (112 km. from Genova). This sprawling naval city at the end of its large gulf features dockyards, marine repair sheds and tanker terminals. One might pause to see the Museo Tecnico Navale (Naval Museum), just inside the Navy Yard, with its collection of old ships and artefacts. But be warned: some of the people who've gazed upon the bewitched, barebreasted figurehead of Atalanta, found floating in the Atlantic Ocean and brought here in 1864, have fallen enchanted. She is "credited" with four suicides to date, including that of a young German naval officer in 1944.

A spectacular corniche drive takes you on to **Portovenere,** a beautiful and distinctively different spot for a holiday. The 7,000 inhabitants live in houses jammed tightly side by side on the hillside often seven stories high and only three yards wide. Each house has been painted in a different colour and manages in other subtler ways to be different

Level-headed woman descends steps with equilibrium; Portovenere, the site of Byron's famous swim.

from its neighbours, as if preserving an independence. Portovenere is a maze of tiny alleyways all going up or down —it seems impossible to find even one along a level. At the harbour, a fish market does brisk business with the daily catch brought in by local vessels.

There are poetic allusions: a plaque cites the "bravery" of Lord Byron in facing the sea's terrors by swimming from here across the Gulf of La Spezia to Lerici.

Walking up a recently refurbished path of dolomite limestone to Portovenere's wild and rocky promontory, you'll find the simple, Gothic church of **San Pietro.** It's on the site of a paleo-Christian church, presumably 5th century, and there are even traces of an earlier pagan temple. The black and white stone interior is striking. Beautiful view!

Portovenere's other church, the 12th-century San Lorenzo, is a much grander affair, again using black and white marble to great effect. You'll see a hollowed-out beam of wood, three yards long. It is said to have washed ashore on Good Friday 1,200 years ago filled with relics of the Crucifixion, bones of martyrs and other precious religious objects. In

the left-hand chapel of the presbytery, a triptych of the *Crucifixion* dates to the 5th century. The church also contains other antique treasures— vestments of multi-coloured silks, brocades and damasks, and cups and boxes of carved and painted ivory—which supposedly arrived in the beam.

Aside from its ancient religious aura, Portovenere offers interesting walks around its rocky coastline, grottoes and coves where one can sunbathe on flat slabs or dive into the sea. For more conventional bathing, take a very short boat ride to the offshore islands of PALMARIA or TINO. Other boat trips go across the bay to Lerici or along the coast to the villages of the Cinque Terre. A *motoscafo* (water taxi) will take you to the Grotta Azzurra, where shimmering blue light encourages fantasy, and around Isola del Tino.

While Byron is said to have swum over to **Lerici,** you'll need to take the coast road around and through La Spezia. This popular town (12 km. from La Spezia) faces its own

Visitors usually agree that the Ligurians are most hospitable.

bay with precipitous hills at its back ensuring warm winter temperatures. Terraces descend quickly to a promenade, and there is ample sheltered mooring for medium-sized pleasure craft. The tall, tile-roofed houses are painted a variety of pastel shades. Though the centre has no beach, sand and swimming can be found either at a northwest-end *lido* or in a cove to the southeast called Eco del Mare. Unusually for this part of the Riviera, the beaches slope gradually into the water. On the most prominent point of Lerici jutting into the sea beyond the jetty is a castle, built in the 13th century by the Pisani, now a youth hostel. A walk round its lower walls gives a panoramic view of the gulf. Worth a visit are the paintings and a Maragliano *Madonna* in the baroque church of San Francesco. The English poet Shelley lived on the Lerici coast before his death by drowning near Viareggio.

The Riviera di Levante ends at the Val (valley) di Magra where the region of Tuscany begins. Inland from Lerici in the valley lies the busy commercial centre of **Sarzana,** a charming and historically important town founded in the 10th century. At its cathedral, **Santa Maria Assunta,** you can admire a Romanesque painting in the form of a cross by Maestro Guglielmo, *The Crucifixion* (1138). A phial said to have contained Christ's blood, called the relic of the Most Precious Blood, has been kept in the cathedral for about 800 years. In 1353, envoys of the pope, Italian princes and other regional leaders symbolically blunted their swords against the column plinths in front of this relic before signing a universal peace agreement. Other notable sights in and around Sarzana: the Cittadella Medicea, local artist Fiasella's *The Calling of St. James and St. John* in the parish church of Sant'Andrea, the arched courtyard of the Palazzo Municipale and the Fortezza di Sarzanello.

Carrara

Michelangelo did it, and so should you. The great sculptor used to go up into the Apuan mountains around Carrara to gaze at the glowing beauty of marble now famous around the world. You can get there easily by car, train (the Turin–Rome line to Marina di Carrara and then a short bus or taxi ride) or on a coach excursion from La Spezia or Marina di Massa.

The road to Bergiola offers a particularly spectacular pano-

Michelangelo's favourite marble quarries remain an awesome sight.

rama of the marble quarries. What looks at first like a glacier turns out to be billions of shimmering marble chips. In Michelangelo's day, chisels and wooden wedges were used to hew out chunks of the ageless crystalline substance. Nowadays explosives open the natural cracks between the faces so the marble may more easily be extracted for cutting.

Along the road to the quarries of COLONNATA, PIASTRA or GRAGNANA, stop at any artisan's shop. You'll find a vast range of marble objects in hues ranging from terra cotta through green, solid blue-grey, pure unveined white and even black. During the winter, quarry workers use diamond-tipped saws and lathes to fashion delicate bowls and dishes, substantial vases and tasteful statuettes, carved and polished chess sets and boards. Here, at least, the word "souvenir" carries no bad taste!

In the marble yards at Carrara you can watch experts with mallets and chisels, calipers and **79** modern air drills, carving the marble pieces that have become familiar far afield. Other yards specialize in cutting marble slices for steps, building façades or floor tiling.

Pisa

The irony is that fame came to this city straddling the river Arno because of an engineering error. For centuries, visitors have flocked to Pisa to see its architectural oddity, the **Leaning Tower** *(Torre Pendente)*.

When Bonnano Pisano and Tedescho bent over their drawing boards around 1172 and designed the cylindrical campanile, or bell-tower, they planned a ground floor, six stories of open loggia and then the bell chamber. But by the time they got to the third cornice, it became obvious that the foundations were inadequate. Work was abandoned. A century later, Giovanni di Simone resumed, lightening the weight on the leaning side and modifying the inclination. By 1350 the bell chamber with seven bells had been added by Tommaso di Andrea—though, nowadays, to avoid vibration, they are never tolled. About 250 years later, Galileo, Pisa's leading luminary, is supposed to have used the tower to demonstrate the principles of gravity. You might think that tilt has been defying gravity ever since.

Approximately 180 feet high, the white marble tower leans about 14 feet to one side. And, yes, it is still falling—at a rate of 0.8 millimetre every year. To this day countless experts and amateurs continue proposing solutions to "save" the famous curiosity.

Seeing is believing, but climbing is better. Though the steps are steep, the view from on high is worth it. Don't forget to ascend the final tiny circular stairs of well-worn marble to the very top of the bell chamber. You can go up the tower any day of the year, until they finally decide it's going to topple.

The reason for the Leaning Tower's existence is the adjacent **cathedral** *(Duomo)*, a beautiful and unusual building begun by Buscheto in 1062 and completed a half century later by Rainaldo. Composed of different shades of marble, the cathedral harmoniously blends classical, paleo-Christian, Byzantine and Arabic motifs in

80

Pisa's tower—still standing, but leaning a tiny bit more each year.

its Romanesque architecture. The local saint Raineri inspired the magnificent bronze doors now no longer used. You'll see beautiful mosaics over the main altar, and each transept altar has a painting (unfortunately cracking) by Andrea del Sarto, half way along the nave. Over the main altar, too, you'll admire Giambologna's *Crucifix* carved from gleaming black marble. Giovanni Pisano's fine pulpit, destroyed by fire, has been reconstructed from the original fragments. Nearby hangs the lamp of Galileo with its intertwined cherubs. Legend claims that the physicist-astronomer formulated his pendulum laws by watching its swing, but in fact, the lamp was cast after Galileo had resolved that problem.

The other noteworthy building on the Piazza del Duomo (it's also called the Piazza of the Miracles), is the circular **Baptistery** *(Battistero)*. Begun in 1152 by Diotisalvi, it has a light and airy interior, famous for the echo. Be sure to see Guido Bigarelli da Como's font with its marvellously detailed inlaid reliefs.

A door through the piazza's north wall leads to the Campo Santo, a cemetery still used today for very important people. Legend says the soil came from Mount Calvary and was blessed by the Lord.

Once Pisa was a totally walled city; now only parts of the fortifications remain to hint at the struggles which ravaged this plain between mountain and sea. And in this former maritime centre, Pisans build ships no more: the Arno is too shallow. Long a proudly independent domain, Pisa fell under Florentine domination at the beginning of the 15th century and was absorbed into Medici-ruled Tuscany. Architecture, painting and sculpture remain to recall the great days.

Pisa is full of interesting churches. Walking from the Duomo down Via Roma and along Via Crispi to Piazza Vittorio Emmanuele II and back along the Corso Italia to the Arno's banks, you'll find half a dozen varying in decoration and style. Across the river the Museo Nazionale displays Pisan artists' work and a fascinating collection of printed matter.*

Pisa lies 75 kilometres to the south of La Spezia on the A12 *autostrada*. Via Aurelia also passes through the city, as do trains from La Spezia on the Turin–Genoa–Rome line.

***

* For more about Pisa and Tuscany, consult the Berlitz guide to FLORENCE in this same series.

What to Do

Relaxing After Hours

If seaside rigours, cultural sightseeing and watching the local bowls *(bocce)* or football *(calcio)* match haven't exhausted you, there are assorted activities to choose from when the Riviera sun goes down. Don't miss firework celebrations marking various local saints' days. Concerts are performed not only in Genoa and San Remo but in out-of-the-way places such as Cervo, where the square outside San Giovanni Battista church provides a magical setting. Each village has its cinema with films in Italian—a chance to improve your knowledge of the language. Some towns have nightclubs and variety shows. Dances are held at many spots along the coast with music to suit people of all ages and inclinations. And late-night discos play predictable top-of-the-pops.

For those eager to try their luck, there's a casino at San Remo (open 2 p.m. to 2 a.m.) with a nightclub and dinner dancing.

Nervi holds an International Ballet Festival in July, which has first-class productions.

Festivals and Other Holidays

Liguria has its share of festivals in honour of saints and assorted other causes. Always colourful, often noisy, they're usually worth going out of the way to see.

Jan. 17	**Chiavari:** Annual handicrafts fair. Look for the macrame, long-fringed, braided lace work and towels.
End January	**San Remo:** Song Festival.
Mardi Gras	**San Remo:** Carnaval with parade of flowers.
End March	**San Remo:** International Jazz Festival.
May 2nd Sunday	**Camogli:** La Sagra del Pesce. Fish cooked outdoors in an enormous pan are served free to all.
June 24	**Genoa:** Procession and fireworks to celebrate the day of St. John the Baptist, patron saint of Genoa.
July	**Nervi:** Ballet Festival.
July and August	**Cervo:** Chamber Music Festival (see p. 45).
July 2	**Loano:** Procession of boats and blessing of the sea.
July, 1st weekend	**Rapallo:** Fireworks and candles floating in the water.
August (1st Sunday)	**Camogli:** Madonna Stella Maris celebrations, with a procession of boats. In the evening, small candles are floated out onto the water.
August 14	**Lavagna:** Feast of the Fieschi, when cakes *(torta)* are given out.
Mid-August	**Portovenere:** Festival of the White Madonna with a medieval pageant.
August 15	**Alassio:** Ferragosto celebrations of the Muretto di Alassio, a wall of tiles on which famous names are engraved.
August 29	**Camogli/San Fruttuoso:** Cristo degli Abissi. Boats and divers go out to this submarine statue.
September (4th Sunday)	**Molini di Triora** (in hills above Taggia): Snail Festival.

Museums

Genoa

Galleria di Palazzo Bianco, Via Garibaldi 11. Closed Sunday afternoons and Mondays. Good collection of Genoan, Dutch and Flemish painters (see p. 22).

Galleria di Palazzo Rosso, Via Garibaldi 18. Closed on Sunday afternoons and Mondays. Portraits by Van Dyck, Dürer and others (see p. 24).

Galleria Nazionale di Palazzo Spinola, Piazza Pelliceria. Closed on Saturdays and Sundays. Italian and Flemish art, furniture and interiors (see p. 24).

Pisa

Museo Nazionale, Piazzetta S. Matteo. Closed on Sunday afternoons and Mondays. Medieval Italian painting and sculpture.

La Spezia

Museo Tecnico Navale (Marine Museum), Piazza Domenico Chiodo. Open daily. Ships, weapons, amphorae, etc.

Savona

Pinacoteca Civica, Via Guardo Superiore 7. Closed on Sundays and Mondays (see p. 31).

Sestri Levante

Pinacoteca Rizzi. Closed on Sunday afternoons. Raphael, Tiepolo, Caravaggio and others.

Monaco

Oceanographic Museum (see p. 56).

Sports

Sunning and Swimming

Wherever you holiday along the Riviera you'll find life inclining naturally to the sea, the beach and the sun. With countless pleasure boats and pedal boats, waders, swimmers, snorkellers, water-skiers and people just floating on inflated mattresses, it's a busy coastal scene. But the sea is wide and there's room for everybody, even though the deck chair you rent may be five rows from the water's edge.

Some resorts have fine sand beaches stretching for kilometres. At others, sand mixed with shingle offers good hunting for collectors of coloured pebbles. Elsewhere, you'll find only stones along the sea. Or there many be no beach at all, but flat rocks useful for both sun bathing and diving. Obviously, the degree of water pollution varies along the coast and from

An angler's patience can be well rewarded in quiet inland streams.

beach to beach. In any event, avoid Genoa and other industrial centres. There are also many pools.

Swimming itself is free. Getting to it may not be: some concessionaires charge an entrance fee to sections of beaches where they rent out deck chairs, umbrellas, mattresses and pedal boats. Beach charges at more sophisticated resorts can be very high. But some hotels arrange for lower weekly or fortnightly rates.

Boating and Water-Skiing

Practically everywhere, you'll find sailing dinghies for hire and someone to teach you the ropes. Motor boats can usually be obtained by the half day at varying and often negotiable prices. A water-skiing session behind a speedboat can be arranged at most resorts.

permission. In areas where submarine archaeology is underway, nothing should be disturbed since the location could help determine the shape of an old Roman vessel, for example. (You'll see many amphorae discovered by divers, at the Naval Museum in Albenga).

Fishing

Though these waters no longer can be called bountiful, you can always try your luck with a rod and reel or underwater with a spear (at Zoagli, Bordighera, Nervi). If you're a trout fisherman, head for the hills.

Golf

With your home club membership card, you can easily arrange to play during your holiday. Green fees are not too expensive. Generally the clubs can be hired and caddies if not golf carts are available. Rapallo, San Remo and Garlenda (near Alassio) have 18-hole golf courses. Arenzano has a 9-hole course.

Tennis

You'll find courts for hire all along the Ligurian coastline for this ever more popular sport. Courts are often under the jurisdiction of local tennis clubs, most of which encourage

Snorkelling and Scuba Diving

Snorkelling is rewarding at many Riviera points—especially at offshore islets. There are many sub-aqua clubs with equipment for hire and instructors who will teach you the rudiments of scuba (self-contained underwater breathing apparatus). Note that any archaeological find must be declared and may not be removed from the water without holiday membership with payment of a reduced fee.

Riding and Walking

Many resorts along the coast offer the possibility of hiring a horse. Some of the better known are Alassio, Arma di Taggia, Chiavari, Finale Ligure, Imperia, La Spezia, Rapallo, San Remo and Sestri Levante. If you prefer exploring on foot, you'll find wonderful paths around the promontory of Portofino, the region behind Diano Marina and along the Cinque Terre and in the mountains, around Torriglia, for example. The local tourist office should be able to give you information about walks in the area.

Skiing

Believe it or not, you can also ski in Liguria. The leading winter sports centres are Monesi (3,000 ft.), Santo Stefano d'Aveto (3,000 ft.) and Sassello (1,200 ft.).

Shopping

Though Liguria itself produces few outstanding items to buy, you'll have your pick at the larger resorts and towns of the specialities that make Italy one of the world's best shopping spots. Genoa's Via XX Settembre and Via Roma, and Savona's Via Paleocapa are the Riviera's major shopping streets. At chic resorts like San Remo and Portofino, the quality may be very high, but so are the prices.

The ceramics in Savona and Albisola can be collectors' items, and as such are not excessively expensive. Some of the unusually shaped dishes could make memorable table centrepieces. Handmade and decorated tiles are also a good buy. The town of Bussana Vecchia is worth investigating for art and handicrafts.

From omnipresent olive wood comes a variety of gift possibilities, the handiest probably bottle openers. Salad bowls, serving dishes, forks and spoons are also popular. Caned wooden chairs are a speciality of Chiavari.

If you're planning to do some hiking and haven't the proper shoes, shop around in the back country for a pair of cleated mountain boots, handcrafted and seemingly indestructible.

Checking prices at home before your holiday will almost certainly demonstrate that you'll do better shopping on the Riviera for typical Italian items. But even if shops confidently pledge to mail your purchases for you, avoid sending things: Italy's postal problems seem to be endless.

Worth Buying

Gold and silver filigree jewellery: very typical of the region, especially Campo Ligure.

Lace: the women of Santa Margherita Ligure and Portofino are noted for their fine craftmanship. The best macrame comes from Chiavari.

Leather: gloves, shoes, bags, belts, luggage, jackets, accessories. Note that Italian shoes have no A, B, C sizes.

Silk: dresses, blouses, shirts, suits, scarves, neckties by name designers or mass produced.

Velvet: handwoven by the women of Zoagli has an international reputation. The small panels set in silk make perfect cushion covers.

Wrought iron articles: a speciality of Sarzana.

Miscellaneous: knitwear, straw goods, costume jewellery, Italian antiques (not Italianate and only if you're knowledgeable) are worth looking at.

Approach with Caution

Cameras, radios, tape recorders and other electronic equipment; tobacco products; all foreign luxury goods, "authentic" religious relics or archaeological items.

Markets

Almost every town and village of Liguria has its weekly market, usually a colourful and animated affair, selling local produce, clothes, kitchen utensils or whatever. San Remo is known for its flower market on Friday mornings. The market of Ventimiglia, very popular with the French (also on Fridays) specializes in clothing. If you're interested in old things, don't miss the antique fair of Taggia, the fourth Saturday and Sunday of the month.

Buying Food

Shopping for the family's immediate consumption can be very exciting. It's most fun—and rewarding—at the outdoor markets which abound on the Riviera. The variety and fresh condition of fruit and vegetables often astound foreign visitors. Crisp green and purple artichokes, red, red tomatoes of various shapes and sizes, to say nothing of plump peaches and juicy strawberries. You'll also find many delicious cooked meat sausages, pâtés and terrines for picnics.

As everywhere in Italy, cheese is a good buy; it may be hard and *piccante,* soft and *dolce,* blue, orange, yellow or white. Much is locally made from ewe's milk. Caravans selling nothing but dozens of types of cheese travel from town to town.

Reflecting the sad condition of the Mediterranean in recent years, fish tends to be scarce in the shops and rather expensive. Your best bet is to find out where the fishermen land their catch and buy from the stalls set up by the wives or at the outdoor market.

While you're browsing, you might want to pick up useful everyday Italian kitchen items not always available abroad: those small aluminium *espresso* coffee makers or garlic squeezers, for example. Or how about a pasta machine?

Whether you're buying outdoors or in small shops (except food or state monopoly items like tobacco), try bargaining a bit—a traditional Italian pastime.

Colourful vegetables and persuasive sellers make marketing fun.

Wining and Dining

You'll have every chance to enjoy that amiable Italian custom of lingering at the table at outdoor and indoor restaurants along the Riviera. Meals —generally of three or four courses—are considered an occasion. Service is normally excellent with a good deal of interplay between the staff and the diners. You'll doubtless get even more attention if you try out whatever Italian you know.

Ligurian chefs take advantage of the abundant supply of fresh vegetables and herbs grown locally. Fats are used sparingly, aside from the thin, golden olive oil from the Imperia area. Sadly, seafood is no longer plentiful on the Riviera (even the mussels come mostly from Barcelona), and when it appears on menus, prices are painfully high.

First Courses

The standard antipasto will be a plate of cold meats such as salami, *mortadella* sausage, ham and roast beef. More substantially, beans and onions (*fagioli e cipolle*) are a popular starter. If you're looking for a bit of adventure, try one of these local specialities: marinated small fish with onions in sauce (*zeri in carpione*); omelet of tiny whitebait (*frittelle di bianchetti*); flat, long shellfish, known locally as "spaghetti of the sea", cooked in oil and garlic (*cappa lunga,* or *cannolicchio*); dried cod simmered with carrots, tomatoes, celery, parsley, garlic, onions, anchovies, mushrooms and pine nuts (*buridda,* a name derived from Arabic); fish salad arranged in a pyramid with cold vegetables in a parsley sauce (*cappon magro*); or cold veal roll stuffed with brains or sweetbreads, pistachios, peas, cheese and marjoram (*cima ripiena*).

A special treat is the *torta pasqualina*—a pie filled with vegetables, eggs and cheese. More traditionally, pasta is, of course, on every menu. Specialities of this region include *piccagge, trenette, lasagne* and *pansoti,* a sort of ravioli stuffed with herbs, eggs and ricotta and served with a walnut cream sauce.

Dishes with *marinara* or *pescatore* in their names feature a savoury sauce of tomato, sea-

Gastronomic adventures await you on the bountiful shores of Liguria.

ed in a mortar. It's usually served over *trenette, lasagne* or *troffie* (a small light potato dumpling). Since basil is a powerful herb, some people recommend that this dish be eaten only at lunchtime—to avoid a sleepless night!

Among soups you'll find the familiar multi-vegetable *minestrone*, Liguria's *zuppa pescatore* called *ciuppin*, a rich broth of stockfish and shellfish, and the *zuppa di datteri*, with razor clams.

Main Courses

Throughout Italy veal *(vitello)* is the principal meat, with lamb *(agnello)*, beef *(manzo* or *bistecca)* and pork *(maiale)* less extensively available. Veal cutlets come in a variety of disguises, breaded or plain, grilled unadorned or with sauces. Chicken *(pollo)* and turkey *(tacchino)* appear frequently on menus. *Pollo alla genovese* is a casserole with potatoes and tomatoes. Local specialities include *pesce al cartoccio*, fish baked with oil, herbs and perhaps a hint of garlic in sealed aluminium foil, *moscardini affogati*, baby squid cooked in their own ink with basil and tomato.

food, peppers, parsley, garlic, wine and capers. *Risotto alla marinara* may be rice cooked with baby cuttlefish *(seppia)*.

Mixed green and white *tagliatelle (paglia e fieno)* often comes with a cream sauce. *Sugo di carciofi*, made of artichokes, fried mushrooms and tomatoes, is also served over pasta.

Don't miss the local speciality, *pesto* or *Genovese* sauce: basil, olive oil, pine nuts, pecorino cheese, garlic, all pound-

As an accompaniment you'll want to sample some vegetables like fried young marrow *(zuc-*

chini fritti), spinach *(spinaci)*, fennel *(finocchio)*, broccoli or mushrooms *(funghi)*.

Cheeses and Desserts

Unless you ask for it, cheese won't be served after a meal, though the board, when it comes, will offer a tempting variety. The *gorgonzola* and *bel paese* you'll find here are infinitely softer and tastier than that exported under refrigeration. Try also *pecorino,* a hard, mature, piquant cheese of ewe's milk, or *ricotta,* soft and often homemade, also from ewe's milk. An unusual item is *formagetto sott'olio,* ewe's-milk cheese sometimes sprinkled with herbs and strong pepper and stored in delicate local olive oil.

Every region of the Italian Riviera specializes in some form of cake or pastry. You'll find *amaretti* (macaroons), a speciality of Savona province, *ravioli dolci* from Genoa, *spungata,* mixed pastries from La Spezia, *castagnole,* pastries of chestnuts, chocolate and sugar from Imperia province, and *chinotti di Savona,* bitter oranges steeped in alcohol. *Baci* (kisses) *di Alassio* are delicious little cakes. *Farinata,* a roast flat-cake made of corn and chickpea flour, is often eaten as a mid-morning snack.

Coffee

Coffee is the almost universal ending to an Italian meal. If you order simply *caffè,* espresso will arrive, strong and black. To get "white" coffee ask for a *cappuccino* which will be in a larger cup or glass topped with a milk froth and sometimes dusted with cinnamon or chocolate. Or you can request *caffè con latte a parte* (with separate milk). Ordering *caffè corretto* will produce black coffee with a shot of *grappa* or other brandy in it.

Wines and Liquor

Every Riviera restaurant offers a good variety of wines, usually including such internationally known names as Chianti, Soave, Lambrusco, Barolo and Valpolicella. Though not many of the wines of Liguria itself are exported, they're excellent. Three have a DOC, a government mark of quality. They are *Rossese di Dolceacqua,* a ruby-red wine produced in Imperia province; *bianco delle Cinque Terre,* a white wine; and *Sciacchetrà* (pronounced shack-ay-trah), a sweet dessert wine, also from the Cinque Terre region, produced by letting the grapes dry in the sun.

For a rewarding drinking experience, ask in any restaurant

or bar if the wine is *sfuso* (i.e. local, usually served in a carafe). The *Vermentino* of Bussana, the *Rossese* and *Pigato* in the Albenga hinterland and the *Pigato* of Ortovero in Savona province deserve particular mention, but wine lovers will compile their own lists of favourites.

As in most Mediterranean countries, you can order some mineral water with your meal, fizzy *(gasata)* or still *(naturale)*. The digestive qualities will be elaborately described on the label of your bottle.

After a meal, the waiter may suggest a liqueur as a further aid to digestion. There are many regional types of *amaro* (meaning bitter) and *amaretto* (made of almonds), which is sweeter and usually pale straw in colour. Try the *amaretto* of Sassello or Portofino.

Places and Prices

The range is from de luxe hotel or yacht-club restaurants to simple snack bars. The standard system of grading eating places takes as much account of the quality of the cutlery, tablecloths and ambiance as of the cuisine: five forks don't necessarily mean superior eating, though they usually indicate big bills. That view over the sea may be delightful; you'll find it's often also costly. Try the back streets or the hinterland if you're economizing. Moreover, to find local specialities you have to seek out

Sorting out Spaghetti

Despite the popular belief that Marco Polo brought pasta back from China in 1292, it was probably the Italians who invented their national dish after all. It turns out that a Genoese soldier mentioned a "basket filled with macaroni" in his will 13 years earlier and that a Ravenna friar wrote of "noodles with cheese" in his chronicle in 1280.

Nor is it true that spaghetti eaten in normal quantities is fattening. True spaghetti contain the embryo of the germ of durum wheat and is positively healthy.

Some of pasta's countless shapes have affectionate names such as butterflies *(farfalle)* and little bow ties *(cravattine)*. It may be coloured green with spinach, as in *fettuccine verdi*. You'll learn much more at a fascinating spaghetti museum in Pontedassio. (Contact the Agnesi pasta firm of Imperia for a visit.)

The most modern machines try to equal mamma's home-made pasta.

the *trattorie* rather than the fancy establishments.

Although you can always find somewhere to eat, most restaurants usually serve lunch between 12.30 and 3, dinner from 7 to 9.30, later at tourist-frequented establishments. All restaurants must close one day a week *(riposo settimanale)*.

In the Italian equivalent of the snack bar, a *tavola calda* (literally "hot table"), you make your choice from dishes displayed behind glass. Prices for such things as omelets, herb pancakes, pizza or fried octopus rings are often by weight—so much per *etto* (100 grams). Enthusiasm for indivi-dual specialities here may result in a final bill higher than for a regular meal elsewhere.

All restaurants impose a cover *(coperto)* charge varying from a few hundred to 1,500 lire. The bill will also normally include a charge of 8 to 12 per cent for VAT (I.V.A. in Italy), plus a service charge *(servizio)* of up to 15 per cent. Thus, 4,000 lire worth of food and wine can cost about 6,500 lire. It's wise always to consider any menu item as 50 per cent more expensive than its listed price, to avoid arguments that could ruin the memory of a pleasant meal (or your di-gestion).

To Help You Order...

I'd like a table.	**Vorrei un tavolo.**
Could we have a table outside?	**Potremmo avere un tavolo all'esterno?**
Do you have a set menu?	**Avete un menù a prezzo fisso?**
I'd like a/an/some...	**Vorrei...**

ashtray	**un portacenere**	fish	**del pesce**
beer	**una birra**	fork	**una forchetta**
bread	**del pane**	fruit	**della frutta**
butter	**del burro**	glass	**un bicchiere**
coffee	**un caffè**	ice-cream	**un gelato**
cream	**della panna**	knife	**un coltello**
dessert	**un dessert**	meat	**della carne**

milk	**del latte**	salad	**dell'insalata**
mineral water	**dell'acqua minerale**	salt	**del sale**
		soup	**una minestra**
napkin	**un tovagliolo**	spoon	**un cucchiaio**
olive oil	**dell'olio d'oliva**	sugar	**dello zucchero**
pepper	**del pepe**	tea	**un tè**
potatoes	**delle patate**	wine	**del vino**

...and Read the Menu

aglio	garlic	**gnocchi**	dumplings
agnello	lamb	**insalata**	salad
albicocche	apricots	**lamponi**	raspberries
al forno	baked	**mela**	apple
anguilla	eel	**melanzana**	aubergine (egg-plant)
anguria	watermelon		
anitra	duck	**merluzzo**	cod
antipasto	hors d'œuvre	**peperoni**	peppers, pimentos
arancia	orange		
arrosto	roast	**pesca**	peach
braciola	chop	**pesce**	fish
branzino	sea bass	**polenta**	purée of maize (cornmeal)
calamari	squid		
carciofi	artichokes	**pollo**	chicken
cipolle	onions	**pomodoro**	tomato
coniglio	rabbit	**prosciutto**	ham
cozze	mussels	**(e melone)**	(with melon)
crostacei	shellfish	**risotto**	rice dish
dentice	dentex (a white fish)	**salsa**	sauce
		sarde	sardines
		seppia	cuttlefish
fagiano	pheasant	**sogliola**	sole
fegato	liver	**spigola**	sea bass
fichi	figs	**spinaci**	spinach
formaggio	cheese	**tartufo**	truffle
fragole	strawberries	**triglia**	red mullet
fritto	fried	**trippe**	tripe
frutti di mare	seafood	**uova**	eggs
		vitello	veal
funghi	mushrooms	**vongole**	clams
gamberi	scampi, prawns	**zuppa**	soup

99

How to Get There

From the United Kingdom, Eire

BY AIR: Many regular flights for Liguria leave London daily and fly directly to Genoa or stop en-route at Milan. Cheaper "tourist" fares with a one-month validity, six-day minimum stay, are also available from April 1 to October 31.

APEX fares for a 14- to 90-day stay cost only a fraction of the regular fares but are subject to several restrictions. The flights leave from certain major English and Scottish cities.

Fly-drive schemes for a seven-day minimum stay (for two or more adults) can be obtained at the same rate as the tourist fare. Full-time **students** (aged 12–26) and young people between 12 and 21 may obtain a 25 per cent reduction on any fares. You can obtain information from individual airlines.

On domestic flights (within Italy) there are reductions of up to 50 per cent if husband and wife travel together with children, and 30 per cent if you travel at night.

BY TRAIN: The route from Calais, Dunkirk or Boulogne takes you through Paris and Turin to Genoa, or via the French Riviera to Ventimiglia.

Return tickets are twice the price of a single to anywhere in Italy from Great Britain; they are valid for two months. Children's reductions differ from country to country, so your ticket agent will have to calculate the fare according to your route.

Travel-at-will tickets *(Biglietti turistici di libera circolazione)* are sold outside Italy and allow unlimited travel on any Italian train for a flat rate, valid for limited lengths of time (8, 15, 21 and 30 days). *Chilometrico* tickets are valid for 3,000 kilometres and can be used by up to five people at the same time.

BY BUS: Europabus, the motor-coach system of the European Railways, co-operates with other European bus companies to run many bus services to Italy from Antwerp, Brussels and other cities, usually from May to September. There are also frequent daily bus services from Milan to Genoa.

BY CAR: From May to September you can transport your car by train from Paris or Boulogne to Milan (contact the French Railways, 179 Piccadilly, London W.1, tel. 01-499 9333). There are good motorways all the way across France and, depending on which route you choose, the passes from France or Switzerland into Italy permit you to connect easily with the *autostrada* to Liguria. Certain passes are closed during the winter months, but among the ones open year-round are the Mont Blanc Tunnel (Chamonix–Aosta) and the Grand Saint Bernard Tunnel (Bourg St. Pierre–Aosta). If you go between May and October it's well worth taking the Simplon Pass from Brig to Domodossola for the breath-taking view.

From North America

BY AIR: Some major cities, such as New York, Montreal and Toronto, offer nonstop flights to Milan which has frequent connecting flights to Genoa.

Excursion fares are worth looking into, such as the APEX (Advance Purchase Excursion) for trips of 14 to 45 days, but the ticket must be bought 30 to 45 days in advance.

There are no student fares from North America to Italy, but the "Italian fare" (for all ages) is available for trips of 14–45 days and 22–60 days, permitting an extra stop-over anywhere in Italy.

101

Charter flights and package tours are readily available from many travel agents. ABC (Advance Booking Charter) offers flights from New York City to Rome with daily connections to Genoa. One-Stop Inclusive Tour Charters (OTC) go to Milan for two-week periods. Group Inclusive Tours (GIT) offer one-week, fly-drive packages (with car provided)—three nights must be spent in Milan, the rest of the time you're free to explore the Riviera.

When to Go

Although the winter months can be fairly rainy, the temperature is never very cold. Winter sports are less than an hour away from the Riviera.

The season when most visitors arrive is, of course, between May or June and September, when the temperature permits bathing. Since every season has its attractions there are usually no changes in hotel rates from summer to winter.

The following charts give approximate monthly averages for temperature and rainfall in Genoa.

		J	F	M	A	M	J	J	A	S	O	N	D
Temperature	°F	50	52	54	57	63	70	73	77	70	63	55	55
	°C	10	11	12	14	17	21	23	25	21	17	13	13
Rainfall	cm.	1	21	8	19	5	2	2	3	9	0	14	4

BLUEPRINT for a Perfect Trip

An A-Z Summary of Practical Information and Facts

Listed after most main entries is an appropriate Italian translation, usually in the singular. You'll find this vocabulary useful when asking for assistance.

Owing to the rapid rate of inflation, all prices mentioned in this book must be regarded as approximate. All the information given here was checked before publication, but changes occur rapidly, and if readers should come across any errors, we would be glad to hear of them.

ACCOMMODATION—see HOTELS

A

AIRPORT *(aeroporto)*. Genoa's Cristoforo Colombo airport (tel. [010] 420.341) has regular flights to Milan, Rome, Zurich and London.

Amenities include a restaurant, snack bar and a currency exchange office, open from 8 a.m. to 7.30 p.m. (closed on Sundays). There is a small duty-free shop. Porters charge a standard 200 lire per bag.

Airline buses operate between the airport and Genoa; their fare is 500 lire one way. A taxi to Genoa will cost you about 3,000 lire.

Porter!	**Facchino!**
Taxi!	**Taxi!**
Where's the bus for…?	**Dov'è l'autobus per…?**

BANKS and CURRENCY EXCHANGE OFFICES *(banca; cambio)*.

B

Banks in Liguria open from 8.20 a.m. to 1.20 p.m., Monday to Friday, except holidays. Exchange offices usually open in the afternoon, too, from 3 to 6.30 p.m. and some operate with variable hours on Saturdays. Exchange offices at Principe and Brignole stations in Genoa are also open on Sunday morning with variable hours.

You should "shop around" when you change your money since currency exchange offices and banks sometimes give different rates on the same day. You may need your passport for identification when changing money.

I want to change some pounds/dollars.	**Desidero cambiare delle sterline/dei dollari.**

B BARBER'S—see HAIRDRESSER'S

BUS SERVICES *(autobus)*. From Genoa, a good bus service goes along the coast and inland. The charge, according to distance, is very reasonable. For example, the fare from Genoa to Rapallo (35 kilometres) is 550 lire. The stops are marked with the sign of the bus company and the word *fermata*.

In Genoa tickets are distributed by machine. A single trip costs 200 lire.

When's the next bus to…?	**Quando parte il prossimo autobus per…?**
Where's the nearest stop?	**Dov'è la fermata più vicina?**
Does this bus go to…?	**Questo autobus va a…?**

C **CAMPING** *(campeggio)*. The Ligurian coastline contains many excellent campsites and parking grounds for caravans (trailers). Amenities vary, and some sites are in particularly picturesque spots. Those along the coast are usually near the water. The Via Aurelia offers better access to them than the motorway.

The yellow pages of the local telephone directory has a section listed *Campeggi, Ostelli, Villaggi Turistici*. Remember—even though you have reservations, it's wise to arrive at the site well before closing time in the summer season.

May we camp here?	**Possiamo campeggiare qui?**
Is there a camp-site near here?	**C'è un campeggio qui vicino?**
We have a tent/caravan (trailer).	**Abbiamo la tenda/la roulotte.**

CAR HIRE *(autonoleggio)*. The major international agencies operate in Liguria, plus a number of smaller local firms which sometimes offer cheaper rates. Some average rates (not including insurance):

Model	per day	plus per kilometre	unlimited mileage (per week)
Fiat 127	9,000 lire	140 lire	150,000 lire
Fiat 131	13,000 lire	170 lire	175,000 lire
Fiat 132 GLS 2000	19,000 lire	200 lire	205,000 lire

A 14 per cent tax is added to all rentals. If you pay by credit card you don't need to leave a deposit. Cheaper weekend arrangements are usually available from 5 p.m. Friday until 9 a.m. Monday.

You must be 25 (21 if you pay by credit card) and hold a valid driver's licence.

I'd like to rent a car…	**Vorrei noleggiare un'automobile…**
tomorrow	**per domani**
for one day	**per un giorno**
for a week	**per una settimana**

CHILDREN. Toddlers are set on a pedestal throughout Italy. Pampered and cossetted, children accompany their parents to cafés and restaurants—even late at night.

There will usually be no difficulty finding a babysitter *(baby-sitter)* as most hotel reception desks keep a list of available sitters or children's nurses. The average fee runs from 1,500 to 3,000 lire per evening plus the evening meal. A qualified children's nurse *(bambinaia)* will ask between 4,000 and 8,000 lire plus the meal.

If your child gets lost, don't worry. Chances are you'll find your smiling youngster in the local police station eating an ice-cream and enjoying centre stage!

Can you get me a babysitter/nurse for tonight?	**Può trovarmi una baby-sitter/ bambinaia per questa sera?**
I've lost my child.	**Ho perso il bambino/la bambina.**

CHURCH SERVICES. Many churches in Liguria possess irreplacable works of art and are locked between services.

Italy is, of course, predominantly Roman Catholic. For mass or confession in English you should ask a priest in any local church or the nearest tourist office. Some English-speaking churches which welcome visitors of all denominations include:

Anglo-American Community Church (St. John's), Via Adua, Alassio.
All Saints' Church, Corso Imperatrice, San Remo.
Anglo-American Community Church, Distacco Piazza Marsala, Genoa (closed June to September).
Israeli Community Synagogue, Via G. Bertora, 6, Genoa.

What time is mass/the service?	**A che ora è la messa/la funzione?**
Do you have mass/services in English?	**C'è la messa/il culto in inglese?**

C

CIGARETTES, CIGARS, TOBACCO *(sigarette, sigari, tabacco)*. In Italy, the sale of tobacco is a government monopoly. All tobacco shops are clearly marked with a large, often illuminated oblong carrying the single letter *T*. Cigarettes are also sold, with government permission, in some bars and hotels. Many Italian brands now use Virginia tobacco and taste similar to British and American cigarettes. Prices range from 650 to 1,200 lire for a packet of 20.

You'll find most European brands of pipe tobacco. Italian cigars may seem strong when compared to foreign brands; non-Italian cigars are also available.

Vietato fumare means no smoking. It's prohibited in buses, some taxis and many public places.

Contraband cigarettes are sold in Genoa near the dock. Sharp-eyed pick-pockets operate in the same area, so perhaps it's better to pull out your wallet in a cigarette shop *(tabacchi* or *tabaccheria)*.

A packet of cigarettes/A box of matches	**Un pacchetto di sigarette/Una scatola di fiammiferi**
with/without filter	**con/senza filtro**

CLOTHING *(abbigliamento)*. Liguria has a temperate winter but from October to March an overcoat may be necessary, as well as when you're in the mountains of the hinterland.

In spring and autumn the days are warm but the nights can turn cool enough for a sweater. Light cotton is a must in the summer.

When going into town or the village for shopping or when visiting churches, dress appropriately. And never wear bathing suits in restaurants or in town.

In casinos and better hotel dining rooms a tie and jacket are advisable. Elsewhere dress is quite informal for both men and women.

COMPLAINTS *(reclamo)*. Complaining about inadequate facilities or services in Italy is one of the easier ways of wasting your valuable holiday time. Any remarks of this sort will release such a flood of voluble Italian with gestures that you'll wish you hadn't bothered!

To avoid unpleasant situations, observe the cardinal rule of commerce in Italy: come to an agreement in advance—the price, the supplements, the taxes and the services to be received, preferably in writing. If that fails, try appealing to the local tourist office or to the police. Usually the threat of a *denuncia,* or official complaint to the police, will cause another flood of rhetoric but should be effective. In all cases involving money, obtain a receipt *(ricevuta)* indicating each separate item.

CONSULATES *(consolato)*. Citizens of countries not represented locally must turn to their consulates in Milan or embassies in Rome.

Australian consulate: Via Turati, 40, Milan; tel. (02) 638.727; hours: 9 a.m. to 12.30 p.m. and 2 to 5 p.m., Monday to Friday.

British consulate: Via XII Ottobre, 2, Genoa; tel. (010) 564.833; hours: 8.30 a.m. to 12.30 p.m. and 3 to 5.15 p.m., Monday to Friday.

Canadian consulate: Via V. Pisa, 19, Milan; tel. (02) 652.600; hours: 9 a.m. to 12.30 p.m. and 2 to 5 p.m., Monday to Friday.

Irish consulate: Via Donatello, 21, Milan; tel. (02) 273.010; hours: 9 a.m. to noon, Monday to Friday.

New Zealand embassy: Via Zara, 28, Rome; tel. (06) 844.8659; hours: 8.30 a.m. to 12.45 p.m. and 1.45 to 5 p.m., Monday to Friday.

South African embassy: Piazza Monte Grappa, 4, Rome; tel. (06) 35.98.857.

U.S. consulate: Piazza Portello, 6, Genoa; tel. (010) 282.741; hours: 9 a.m. to 12 noon, 2 to 4 p.m., Monday to Friday.

Where is the... consulate?	**Dov'è il consolato...?**
British/American/ Australian/Canadian/Irish	**britannico/americano/ canadese/irlandese**
Where is the New Zealand/ South African embassy?	**Dov'è l'ambasciata della Nuova Zelanda/sudafricana?**

CONVERTER CHARTS. For fluid, tire pressure and distance measures, see page 110. Italy uses the metric system.

Temperature

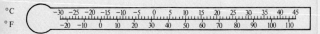

Length

Weight

grams 0   100   200   300   400   500   600   700   800   900   1 kg

oz.   0   4   8   12   1 lb.   20   24   28   2 lb.

CREDIT CARDS and TRAVELLERS' CHEQUES *(carta di credito; travellers cheque)*. Most major hotels in Liguria and many restaurants and shops now accept leading credit cards. Look for the signs displayed on doorways, in lobbies, etc.

Travellers' cheques are generally accepted, though it's advisable to change them at a *cambio* (currency exchange) or at a bank, where you receive a higher rate of exchange than in stores or restaurants.

Do you accept travellers' cheques/credit cards?	**Accetta travellers cheques/ carte di credito?**

CRIME and THEFT *(delitto; furto)*. Around the dock areas of Genoa, Savona and La Spezia shady characters may offer "imported" gold watches or other goods. These deals should be avoided, and the areas, too, after dark.

Otherwise, normal precautions which are necessary in all tourist areas should be taken: never leave objects in view in your car; always lock your hotel room; deposit valuables in the hotel safe. See also POLICE.

I want to report a theft.	**Voglio denunciare un furto.**

CURRENCY *(valuta)*. The *lira* (plural *lire,* abbreviation *L* or *Lit.*) is the unit of Italian currency. Notes are issued in denominations of 500, 1,000, 2,000, 5,000, 10,000, 20,000, 50,000 and 100,000 lire. Coins now in circulation include 10, 20, 50, 100 and 200 lire.

To ease the current coin shortage banks issue a type of banknote called an *assegno al portatore* payable in units of 50, 100, 150, 200, 250 and 350 lire.

Don't be surprised if you receive part of the change for a purchase in telephone tokens *(gettone)* worth 50 lire, or even in sweets.

CURRENCY EXCHANGE—see **BANKS**

CUSTOMS CONTROLS *(dogana)*. See also ENTRY FORMALITIES and DRIVING IN ITALY. The following chart shows what items you may take into Italy duty free:

from:	Cigarettes		Cigars		Tobacco (grams)		Spirits		Wine
EEC	300	or	75	or	400		1 ½	or	3
Europe non-EEC	200	or	50	or	250		¾	or	2
outside Europe	400	or	100	or	500		¾	or	2

Currency restrictions: Though there is no limit to the amount of money in travellers' cheques or foreign currency you may import or export, you are not allowed to carry more than 100,000 lire in Italian currency in either direction. Upon entry you must also fill out a special form, validated by a customs officer, if you expect to re-export more than 200,000 lire when you leave Italy. This does not apply to unendorsed travellers' cheques.

The exportation of works of fine art or antiques requires a certificate, which a legitimate vendor will obtain for you from the Department of Fine Arts. Penalties for unauthorized exportation include confiscation and a fine.

I've nothing to declare.	**Non ho nulla da dichiarare.**
It's for my personal use.	**È per mio uso personale.**

DRIVING IN ITALY

Entering Italy: To bring your car into Italy you will need:

● an international driving licence (non-Europeans)
● car registration papers
● Green Card (an extension to your regular insurance policy, making it valid for foreign countries). Though not obligatory for EEC countries, it's still preferable to have it.
● national identity sticker for your car and the red warning triangle in case of break-down.

Road conditions: An *autostrada* (or motorway) with many tunnels runs along the coast. Each section requires the payment of a toll: You collect a card from an automatic machine and pay at the other end

D for the distance travelled. Try to stock up on 100-lire coins or banknotes, since the toll booth attendants don't like to make change.

The Via Aurelia is a much more scenic but slower route. For those who wish to savour Liguria it's a must.

Driving conditions: Drive on the right, pass on the left. Italian drivers are well-known for speed and panache. Don't rely on traffic lights, since many local drivers tend to anticipate the green and ignore the first few seconds of the red. Keep a sharp watch, at night especially, for small tricycle carts, many of which can be inadequately lighted. Steep drops at the side of mountain roads are not always protected by crash barriers, so keep off the verge (shoulder).

The size of a car's engine determines the speed limit in Italy. Ask for details at the border or when hiring your car. In-town limit: 50 kilometres per hour.

Parking: Parking will always present a problem along the coast. Your best bet is to use the car as little as possible once you arrive at your destination, as buses are cheap and plentiful. Away from the coast you'll have no parking difficulties except in very popular spots.

Fuel and oil: There are plenty of petrol (gas) stations along the Ligurian coastline, but many close for lunch from 12 to 3 p.m. Regular *(normale)* petrol, or 84 octane costs about 480 lire per litre and extra *(super)* or 98 octane, approximately 500 lire. Usually diesel is also available at about 170 lire per litre. Most brands of oil sell for around 1,600 lire per litre.

Anyone entering Italy with foreign licence plates can buy coupons for petrol (not diesel) at a special reduced rate. These can be obtained before leaving in local automobile clubs or at the border. Service stations accepting the petrol coupons display a sign marked "coupons" Unused vouchers may be refunded at the border: either in an office of the A.C.I. *(Automobile Club d'Italia)* or at a branch of the Italian tourist office.

Breakdowns: There are emergency call boxes marked SOS every 2 kilometers along motorways, or call 116 from the nearest telephone box to get in contact with the A.C.I. They will come to your aid for 3,500 lire during the day and 4,500 lire at night. You must produce the fuel card received with petrol coupons at the border upon entry. Italy is a land of garages, but most are acquainted with the Fiat and may have little knowledge of any other car, though that will not prevent them tinkering. Look in the local yellow pages if you have the chance,

to try to find a garage that specializes in your make of vehicle. **D**
Mechanics in smaller towns and villages tend to be more experienced
and adaptable for small repairs not needing new spare parts.

Traffic police *(polizia stradale)*: All towns along the Ligurian coast
have signs posted giving the location and telephone number either of
the Polizia Stradale or the Carabinieri. Ignoring the speed limits and
reckless overtaking (passing) may get you fined on the spot. Protesting
your ignorance of the law or of local signs will do you no good. You
should ask for a receipt for any fines paid.

Fluid measures

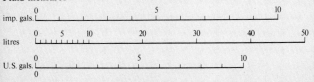

Distance

Road signs: Most road signs employed in Italy are international. But
there are some written signs you might come across, too:

Accendere le luci	Use headlights
Caduta massi	Falling rocks
Curva pericolosa	Dangerous bend (curve)
Deviazione	Diversion (Detour)
Discesa pericolosa	Steep hill (with gradient percentage)
Divieto di sorpasso	No overtaking (passing)
Divieto di sosta	No stopping
Lavori in corso	Road works (Men working)
Parcheggio autorizzato	Parking allowed
Passaggio a livello	Level railway crossing
Pericolo	Danger
Rallentare	Slow down
Senso vietato/unico	No entry/One-way street
Vietato l'ingresso	No entry
Zona pedonale	Pedestrian zone

D

(International) Driving Licence	**patente (internazionale)**
car registration papers	**libretto di circolazione**
Green Card	**carta verde**

Can I park here?	**Posso parcheggiare qui?**
Are we on the right road for…?	**Siamo sulla strada giusta per…?**
Fill her up please, top grade.	**Per favore, faccia il pieno di super.**
Check the oil/tires/battery.	**Controlli l'olio/i pneumatici/**
	la batteria.

| I've had a breakdown. | **Ho avuto un guasto.** |
| There's been an accident. | **C'è stato un incidente.** |

DRUGS. Anyone possessing or selling narcotics in Italy faces a vigorous police force and a stiff penalty. The backlog of cases to be heard in the courts is long, and anyone arrested for a suspected drug offence may spend as much as a year in jail before even being formally charged.

DRY-CLEANING—see **LAUNDRY**

E

ELECTRICITY *(elettricità).* Liguria is changing over to 220-volt current and that's what you will find in all but the oldest establishments. Most electrical outlets are of the two-pin variety, but many hotels have razor sockets which accept either American flat pin or British round pin plugs. If in doubt, consult the hotel receptionist or visit an electrician's.

| an adaptor | **una presa complementare** |
| What's the voltage? | **Qual è il voltaggio?** |

EMBASSIES—see **CONSULATES**

EMERGENCIES *(emergenza).* Depending on the nature of the problem, refer to the separate entries in this section such as CONSULATES, MEDICAL CARE, POLICE etc.

Some useful telephone numbers:

All-purpose emergency number		113
Assistance on the road		116
Emergency medical services	Genoa	54.841
	Imperia	78.930
	La Spezia	34.009
	Savona	806.868

And a few words we hope you'll never need:

Careful!	**Attenzione!**	Police!	**Polizia!**
Fire!	**Incendio!**	Stop!	**Stop!**
Help!	**Aiuto!**	Stop thief!	**Al ladro!**

ENTRY FORMALITIES. See also CUSTOMS CONTROLS and DRIVING IN ITALY. Most visitors, including citizens of Australia, Canada, Eire, New Zealand, the United Kingdom and the U.S.A. need only a valid passport to enter Italy. Tourists from South Africa must have a visa.

GUIDES and INTERPRETERS *(guida; interprete)*. Most leading hotels or the local tourist office can arrange for reliable multilingual guides or interpreters for any occasion. For a group of 1–10 expect to pay 13,000 lire for a half-day or 20,000 lire (plus lunch) for a full day.

We'd like an English-speaking guide.	**Desideriamo una guida che parla inglese.**
I need an English interpreter.	**Ho bisogno di un interprete d'inglese.**

HAIRDRESSER'S and BARBER'S *(parrucchiere; barbiere)*. Most tourist centres in Liguria have beauty salons and hairdressers'. Prices vary according to the style of the establishment and the location, though they can be very reasonable away from the fashionable areas.

Approximate prices		
Man's	haircut *(taglio di capelli)*	2,500 lire
Woman's	cut, hair styling *(taglio)*	5,000 lire
	shampoo and set *(shampo e messa in piega)*	4,000 lire
	rinse *(cachet)*	2,000 lire
	tint *(tinta)*	9,500 lire
	(hair-setting lotions are extra)	

Not too much off (here).	**Non troppo corti (qui).**
A little more off (here).	**Un po' di più (qui).**
a colour chart	**la tabella dei colori**
a colour rinse	**un cachet**

HEALTH—see **MEDICAL CARE**

H **HITCH-HIKING** *(autostop)*. Many people travel by "thumbing" rides all over Italy. It must be pointed out that hitch-hiking is not allowed on motorways.

Can you give me a lift to...? **Può darmi un passaggio fino a...?**

HOTELS and ACCOMMODATION *(albergo; alloggio)*. The difference in official classification depends mainly on the facilities offered. The local Azienda Autonoma di Soggiorno e Turismo keeps a list of rooms to let *(camere da affittare)*, hotels and boarding-houses. There are usually five categories of hotels or *alberghi*.

Approximate rates for a double room without board, summer season:

Luxury	46,000 to 80,000 lire	3rd class	10,000 to 17,000 lire
1st class	25,000 to 60,000 lire	4th class	6,000 to 12,000 lire
2nd class	15,000 to 27,000 lire		

Unless prices are given as *tutto compreso* (all inclusive), as much as 20 per cent in tax and service can be added.

Other possibilities for accommodation include the *pensione,* where you'll get a clean bed with non-connecting bathroom and toilet for 8,000–10,000 lire, and the *locanda,* similar to a *pensione* but usually without a restaurant. There may not be hot water or even a basin in the room in a *locanda,* but the prices are very low (from 6,000 to 8,000 lire).

Though it's possible to rent apartments *(appartamento)* on the Ligurian coast in the summer, they are hard to find and expensive. The rent may not include electricity or heating (necessary in winter). See also YOUTH HOSTELS.

a quiet room **una stanza tranquilla**
a double/single room **una camera matrimoniale/singola**
with/without bath **con/senza bagno**
What's the rate per night? **Qual è il prezzo per una notte?**

I **INTERPRETERS**—see **GUIDES**

L **LANGUAGE.** Many of the people of Liguria speak both standard Italian and a local dialect. And now, with the great influx of tourists some are learning to master English or German.

The Berlitz phrase book ITALIAN FOR TRAVELLERS covers most situations you're likely to encounter in Italy. The Berlitz Italian-English/English-Italian pocket dictionary contains an 8,000-word glossary of each language, plus a menu-reader supplement.

Do you speak English?   **Parla inglese?**

LAUNDRY and DRY-CLEANING *(lavanderia; tintoria or lavaggio a secco)*. Laundries and dry-cleaning establishments abound in Liguria, most offering overnight service and minor repairs.

Following are some typical prices:

Laundry (ironed)		
shirt	600 lire	*camicia*
blouse	700 lire	*camicetta*
set of underclothes	500 lire	*cambio di biancheria intima*
pyjamas	800 lire	*pigiama*
nightgown	700 lire	*camicia da notte*

Dry-cleaning		
dress	1,500 lire	*abito*
skirt (unpleated)	800 lire	*gonna*
sports jacket	1,300 lire	*giacca sportiva*
trousers	1,000 lire	*pantaloni*
sweater	600 lire	*maglione*
blouse	700 lire	*camicetta*

When will it be ready?   **Quando sarà pronto?**
I must have this for tomorrow   **Mi serve per domani mattina.**
morning.

LOST PROPERTY *(oggetti smarriti)*. Check with the Ufficio di Oggetti Smarriti at the local police station and the tourist office, or try to trace lost property through the railway, taxi company, or other.

  It's a good idea to take out property insurance in your own country for the duration of your holiday in Italy. If you lose something on your **115**

L trip, report the loss to the local police and obtain a document to show to your insurance company on your return.

For lost children see the section CHILDREN.

I've lost my passport/wallet/handbag.	**Ho perso il passaporto/portafoglio/la borsetta.**

M **MAIL** *(posta)*. See also POST OFFICE. It's wiser not to plan to get mail during a brief visit to Italy. Hotels and *pensioni* will receive mail for guests, but it may not always be forwarded to another address if it arrives too late. If you must receive mail, have it sent to *Fermo Posta* (poste restante, or general delivery) at the nearest large village or town, quoting the province. Mail should be addressed:

> Jane Smith
> Fermo Posta
> Posta Centrale
> Finale Ligure, Savona
> Italy

You'll need your passport as proof of identity (a driving licence won't be accepted).

Have you received any mail for me?	**C'è posta per me?**

MAPS *(pianta; carta topografica)*. Maps can be found at news-stands, book-shops and some service stations in Liguria. The local tourist information office will give you a map indicating places of interest to the visitor.

Since there has been a good deal of road construction recently along the Ligurian coast, make sure you check the date of the map before buying it.

The maps in this book were prepared by Falk-Verlag, Hamburg, which also publishes a map of Italy.

a street plan of...	**una piantina di...**
a road map of this region	**una carta stradale di questa regione**

MEDICAL CARE. Before you travel abroad on holiday, you are advised to take out appropriate medical insurance, either through your insurance company or your travel agency. British citizens should visit their local Social Security office to procure the required documentation for health treatment in other EEC countries.

Many of the resorts along the Ligurian coast have a public service to deal with emergencies. See Emergencies.

In addition to medicine and other products, pharmacies *(farmacia)* may be able to give temporary aid and advice. One *farmacia* stays open in each town on weekends and public holidays.

a dentist	**un dentista**
a doctor	**un medico**
hospital	**ospedale**
an upset stomach	**il mal di stomaco**
a fever	**la febbre**

MEETING PEOPLE. It's customary to say *buon giorno* (good morning) or *buona sera* (good afternoon/evening) whenever you enter a shop, bar, restaurant or any other establishment. You may be ignored in the din of existing conversation, but don't let that bother you.

Always preface any query with *per favore,* or *per piacere,* both of which mean "please". "Thank you" is *grazie* or *grazie mille* (thank you very much). For "good-bye" you can use the word *arrivederci* (until we meet again) or *ciao,* which is very informal and only for those you know well.

There are two ways of saying "excuse me". If you mean "I didn't hear very well", you say *mi scusi.* "May I please get past you?" is *permesso.* When introduced to someone, you should always shake hands and murmur *piacere* (it's a pleasure).

Even if you take pride in your spoken Italian, the local dialect will defeat you. On the beach, though, you probably won't have that problem since the Italians there are often on holiday from other parts of the country, in a relaxed mood and interested in meeting other people.

NEWSPAPERS and MAGAZINES *(giornale; rivista).* Most villages or towns have at least one news-stand which sells foreign language newspapers and magazines for tourists, though prices are high and deliveries are always at least one day behind publication date. Most also sell newsmagazines.

Have you any English-language newspapers?	**Avete giornali in inglese?**

PHOTOGRAPHY. Surprisingly, the use of an ordinary flash is permitted in most public buildings. You'll also need one for such spectacular sights as the Grotto of Toirano.

Major brands of film are available in the many photographic shops throughout Liguria, though they are often more expensive than elsewhere. You may prefer to take film back home with you for processing, as it usually takes some time on the spot. Never leave a camera in a car, or unattended anywhere.

N.B.: In Italian, *camera* means "room"!

I'd like a film for this camera.	**Vorrei una pellicola per questa macchina fotografica.**
a black and white film	**una pellicola in bianco e nero**
a colour-slide film	**una pellicola per diapositive**
a film for colour prints	**una pellicola per fotografie a colori**
35-mm film	**una pellicola trentacinque millimetri**
super-8	**super otto**

POLICE *(polizia, carabinieri)*. Though police aren't too much in evidence in Liguria, they usually appear when needed.

The Vigili Urbani deal with routine matters of traffic direction, parking and giving advice. Their telephone number in Genoa is 530.101. For more serious matters, e.g. theft, contact the Carabinieri in Genoa, Imperia, La Spezia or Savona at 212.121.

The roads and motorways are patrolled by the Polizia Stradale, often on motorcycle or in plainly marked cars. They can impose a fine on the spot for an offence.

The universal police emergency number is 113.

Where's the nearest police station?	**Dov'è il più vicino posto di polizia?**

POST OFFICE *(posta, ufficio postale)*. See entries MAIL and TELEPHONE. The principal post offices in Liguria are open from 8 a.m. to 8 p.m. Monday to Saturday with late-night telegram services, but the smaller branches usually close at 2 p.m. with telegram services until 8.

Stamps *(francobolli)* are sold over the counter and also at tobacconists *(tabacchi)* and in some hotels. Letters to other parts of Italy should be sent express *(espresso)*, which costs more but generally ensures speedier processing within the sometimes languid mail service. Postcards sent to relatives at home will frequently arrive after you do.

Telegrams *(telegramma)*: Night letters, or letter telegrams, which are slower in arriving than regular telegrams (they are posted to their destination when received, rather than conveyed by express mail or telephone as with regular telegrams) are called *lettera telegramma* in Italian. They can only be sent overseas, and are cheaper than ordinary cables.

A stamp for this letter/postcard, please.	**Per favore, un francobollo per questa lettera/cartolina.**
I want to send a telegram to...	**Desidero mandare un telegramma a...**
express (special delivery)	**espresso**
airmail	**via aerea**
registered	**raccomandata**
poste restante (general delivery)	**fermo posta**

PRICES *(prezzi)*. See also other appropriate headings. The influx of tourists and inflation have combined to make Liguria as expensive as anywhere else to take a holiday, especially in the fashionable resorts.

There are still some bargains though: wine bought in a shop can be as little as 800 lire for a 2-litre bottle, and in many *trattorie* in the side streets you can get a meal for two, including wine, for 9,500 lire.

You should anticipate that a large part of your holiday budget will be spent on incidentals, so plan accordingly. A 12 per cent service charge and/or VAT (tax), is added to many bills. All restaurants charge a *coperto* to cover the tablecloth, napkins and bread which can amount to 1,000 lire per person.

Here are some typical prices in lire:

Continental breakfast	1,000–1,500	Aperitif	600
Lunch ⎱ fairly good	7,000	Gin and tonic	1,000
Dinner ⎰ establishment	10,000	Beer	600
Coffee	500	Soft drink	600

Discotheque (entry and first drink)	3,000–5,000
Cinema	2,500
Museum	0–500

Is there an entry charge?	**Si paga per l'entrata?**
How much?	**Quant'è?**
Have you something less expensive?	**Ha qualcosa di meno caro?**

P **PUBLIC HOLIDAYS** *(festa)*. People in Liguria celebrate the nine Italian public holidays each year plus a number of purely local ones, which vary from place to place. When a holiday falls on a Thursday or Tuesday, some Italians may still take a long week-end, though this practice is no longer common. The week or ten days surrounding *Ferragosto* in August may also see more shops closed than usual.

January 1	*Capodanno* or *Primo dell'Anno*	New Year's Day
April 25	*Festa della Liberazione*	Liberation Day
May 1	*Festa del Lavoro*	Labour Day
August 15	*Ferragosto*	Assumption Day
November 1	*Ognissanti*	All Saints' Day
December 8	*Immacolata Concezione*	Immaculate Conception
December 25	*Natale*	Christmas Day
December 26	*Santo Stefano*	Saint Stephen's Day
Movable date:	*Lunedì di Pasqua*	Easter Monday

Are you open tomorrow?   **È aperto domani?**

R **RADIO and TELEVISION** *(radio; televisione)*. Shortwave reception throughout the late evening and early morning is very good on the Ligurian coast. After dark, the AFN programme from Frankfurt or Munich can often be heard clearly on AM radio (medium wave). The BBC World Service and the Voice of America can be picked up on ordinary transistor radios.

S **SIESTA.** The pace of life slows considerably after one o'clock, when many people leave their offices and shops to take a long lunch "hour" or nap. Though not so rigorously observed as it used to be, siesta is a time for relaxing. Bars and restaurants do their biggest business during this period; most shops and all public offices close.

If you have the energy in the fierce midday sun, this is a good opportunity to get about, since the roads are seldom crowded. At about 4 p.m., life returns to normal.

T **TAXIS** *(tassì* or *taxi)*. Taxis are plentiful all along the coast and may be hailed on the street or a cab rank. The charge is shown on the meter. The yellow pages list taxis you can call by telephone; these vehicles will arrive with a sum already shown on the meter. Many taxi drivers request you not to smoke. It's not usual to tip taxi-drivers unless they have been helpful with baggage or other services.

A 10-kilometre (6-mile) taxi ride will cost around 3,000 to 4,000 lire anywhere on the coast.

What's the fare to...?   **Qual è la tariffa per...?**

TELEGRAMS—see **POST OFFICE**

TELEPHONE *(telefono)*. To make an international call, go to the main post office in the larger towns where there are operator services. Your hotel will also get the number for you, of course, but it will cost a little more. Either way, the long-distance lines are often overloaded, so be prepared for a long wait.

All public phones take tokens *(gettone)* only, which you obtain at a bar for 50 lire each (the barman will buy back any you don't use). Armed with a good quantity of *gettoni,* you can dial direct from a phone booth marked *Interurbane* either abroad or within Italy. See the telephone directory for code numbers. First, insert a *gettone,* lift the receiver, and wait. There may be silence for quite a while before you get the dial tone, a series of regular dash-dash-dash sounds. (A dot-dot-dot sequence means the exchange is overloaded, in which case you must hang up and try again.) If the dot-dot-dot sound breaks in when you are dialling a number, it means that one of the telephone lines along the way is busy so you have to start all over again.

For a transferred-charge (collect) call, specify *chiamata R* (pronounced *kyah-maa-tah ay-ray)*.

A few useful numbers:

Local directory inquiries	12
Other Italian inquiries	181
Operator for Europe and North Africa	15
Operator for western hemisphere and Asia	170

Can you get me this number in...?   **Può passarmi questo numero a...?**

TIME DIFFERENCES. The chart below shows the difference in time between Italy and some selected cities. Since the U.S.A., U.K. and Italy all put the clock ahead an hour in summer, the time difference remains essentially the same all year round.

121

T Summer time chart:

New York	London	**Italy**	Jo'burg	Sydney	Auckland
6 a.m.	11 a.m.	**noon**	noon	8 p.m.	10 p.m.

What time is it? **Che ore sono?**

TIPPING *(mancia)*. For specific recommendations, see inside back cover. "When in doubt, tip" is a fair maxim if you intend to use that particular service again, but don't forget that not leaving a tip is often the only recourse of a dissatisfied customer. A 10 per cent tip will usually suffice.

Many restaurants add a service charge, a fixed percentage to the bill. In that case tips are only offered for special service.

TOILETS *(gabinetti)*. Toilets are found in all restaurants and bars in Liguria (not all towns and villages have public street conveniences). *Donne* or *Signore* (note the final *e*) means "women"; *Uomini* or *Signori* (note the final *i*) for "men".

It's usual to buy at least a coffee if you use the facilities in a bar.

Where are the toilets? **Dove sono i gabinetti?**

TOURIST INFORMATION OFFICES *(agenzia turistica)*. The Ente Provinciale per il Turismo (E.P.T.) operates a central office in each of the four provinces of Imperia, Savona, Genoa and La Spezia. In Genoa their address is: Via Roma 11, 3/4, tel. 581.371.

However, most tourists will usually do business with the Azienda Autonoma di Soggiorno e Turismo located in many towns and villages. They will give you information on hotels and points of interest, and have brochures and maps of the region.

Offices called Pro Loco operate in much the same way but generally speak only Italian. The local *municipio* (town hall) will often have useful information.

Italian State Tourist Offices (in America called Italian Government Travel Offices) are maintained in many countries abroad. Their Italian name is Ente Nazionale Industrie Turistiche, abbreviated E.N.I.T.

United Kingdom: 201, Regent St., London W.1; tel. (01) 734-4631.

U.S.A.: 500 N. Michigan Ave., Chicago, IL 60601; tel. (312) 222-1083. 630 Fifth Ave., New York, NY 10020; tel. (212) 245-4822. 360 Post Street, Suite 801, San Francisco, CA 94108 (415) 392-6206.

Canada: 3, Place Ville-Marie, Suite 22, Montréal 13, P.Q ; tel. (514) 866-7667.

Eire: 47, Merrior Square, Dublin 2; tel. (01) 66397.

Australia and New Zealand: E.N.I.T., c/o Alitalia, 118 Alfred St., Milson Point 20, Sydney; tel. 922 15 55.

South Africa: E.N.I.T., London House, 21 Loveday St., Johannesburg.

TRAINS *(treno)*. A timetable board in a Ligurian railway station looks like some kind of game, with numbers in many colours, stars and symbols of many shapes, useful once you get to know the system!

There are four types of trains, each marked on the board in a different colour, with a colour code beneath them.

Rapido	The best, fastest (and most expensive) train, which may be one-class (de-luxe/first) with all seats reserved and for which a sizeable supplement may be charged.
Direttissimo or *Espresso*	Stops at major cities only; has both first- and second-class coaches (seat reservations are possible in first class).
Diretto	Slower than the *direttissimo,* it makes a number of local stops; first- and second-class coaches.
Locale	A local train which stops at almost every station.

Vagone letto	*Vagone ristorante*	*Cuccette*	*Bagagliaio*
Sleeping-car with 1-, 2- or 3-bedded compartments including washing facilities	Dining-car	Sleeping-berth car *(couchette)* with blankets, sheets and pillows	Luggage van (baggage car); registered luggage only permitted

It's wise to arrive at the station in plenty of time, since rail travel is such a bargain in Italy that trains are often crowded.

All lines converge on Genoa, which has two stations. Principe serves the trains from France, Turin, Milan and Rome. Brignole serves the local lines, many of which also go to Principe. Both stations have

T

porters, taxis and left luggage facilities, as well as snack bars and restaurants.

single (one-way)	**andata**
return (round-trip)	**andata e ritorno**
first/second class	**prima/seconda classe**
When's the best train to...?	**A che ora parte il miglior treno per...?**
I'd like to make a reservation	**Vorrei riservare un posto.**

TRAVELLERS' CHEQUES—see CREDIT CARDS

W **WATER** *(acqua)*. The water of Liguria, most of which comes down from the mountains, is perfectly safe to drink. Nevertheless, the usual custom is to drink bottled water *(acqua minerale)* with a meal.

a bottle of mineral water	**una bottiglia di acqua minerale**
carbonated	**gasata**
non-carbonated	**naturale**

Y **YOUTH HOSTELS** *(ostello della gioventù)*. Liguria has a treat in store for youth hostellers. Several hostels have been established in historic buildings and spectacular locations (in Lerici, the hostel is located in a 13th-century castle high on a promontory with views over the Gulf of La Spezia).

An international membership card from your national youth hostel association is required. Rules are similar to those in Y.H.A.s anywhere and prices are very low.

For information, see the yellow pages of any telephone directory under the heading *Campeggi, Ostelli,* or write to the Associazione Italiana Ostelli della Gioventù, Salita Salvatore Viale, Genoa (tel. [010] 586.407).

DAYS OF THE WEEK

DAYS

Sunday	**domenica**	Thursday	**giovedì**
Monday	**lunedì**	Friday	**venerdì**
Tuesday	**martedì**	Saturday	**sabato**
Wednesday	**mercoledì**		

SOME USEFUL EXPRESSIONS

yes/no	**sì/no**
please/thank you	**per favore/grazie**
excuse me/you're welcome	**mi scusi/prego**
where/when/how	**dove/quando/come**
yesterday/today/tomorrow	**ieri/oggi/domani**
left/right	**sinistra/destra**
big/small	**grande/piccolo**
cheap/expensive	**buon mercato/caro**
open/closed	**aperto/chiuso**
I don't understand.	**Non capisco.**
What does this mean?	**Cosa significa?**
Please write it down.	**Lo scriva, per favore.**
Waiter!/Waitress!	**Cameriere!/Cameriera!**
I'd like...	**Vorrei...**
How much is that?	**Quant'è?**
Where are the toilets?	**Dove sono i gabinetti?**

NUMBERS

0	**zero**	18	**diciotto**
1	**uno**	19	**diciannove**
2	**due**	20	**venti**
3	**tre**	21	**ventuno**
4	**quattro**	22	**ventidue**
5	**cinque**	30	**trenta**
6	**sei**	31	**trentuno**
7	**sette**	32	**trentadue**
8	**otto**	40	**quaranta**
9	**nove**	50	**cinquanta**
10	**dieci**	60	**sessanta**
11	**undici**	70	**settanta**
12	**dodici**	80	**ottanta**
13	**tredici**	90	**novanta**
14	**quattordici**	100	**cento**
15	**quindici**	101	**centouno**
16	**sedici**	500	**cinquecento**
17	**diciassette**	1000	**mille**

Index

An asterisk (*) next to a page number indicates a map reference.

INDEX

INDEX

128